Be*tween* Baby Dolls
and Boyfriends:
How to Successfully Navigate
Your Daughter's Tween Years

Between Baby Dolls
and Boyfriends:
How to Successfully Navigate
Your Daughter's Tween Years

**By Debi Smith-Racanelli, MA, CAGS
and Kendall Racanelli**

First Printing, 2014

ISBN: 978-1501049514
ISBN: 1501049518

Library of Congress Control Number: 2014918468
CreateSpace Independent Publishing Platform, North
Charleston, SC

www.betweenbabydollsandboyfriends.com

To all tween girls and those who love them. Because this book was written by a mom and her tween girl, there is an unavoidable slant toward moms. But we know any dad or other caregiver will get a lot out of this book as well. We dedicate this to you all, and hope that our work will bring you closer together with your tween.

Contents

Introduction: Why the Need for This Book

My daughter Kendall cried every day for two weeks when I dropped her off at the kindergarten door. To get her through this, her teacher allowed me to stand in the line of students, Kendall sniffling and squeezing my hand as the line moved up. When we got to the door where the teacher greeted each student, I would transfer Kendall's hand to hers and then I could leave, knowing she was fine. What I wouldn't give to be able to stand by her and hold her hand through the tween years, confident that I was handing her off to a safe, nurturing place.

Nostalgia will get me nowhere. So in shaking off wistful memories of parenting problems past, I knew that I needed to make a shift in my expectations and approach in guiding Kendall through this new stage in her life known as the tween years. The tween years encompass the years 9-12, in be*tween* the childhood and teenage years.

I have two advanced degrees in psychology, and have worked with parenting issues for more than a decade. But my bigger role is that of mom. And despite my years of theories, poring through research, and clinical practice, being a mom means not having all of the answers. It has been a time full of challenges, doubts, second-guessing, and frustration; but also love, laughter, and triumph.

My intention in writing this book is to do more than just parcel out statistical information and developmental information. I want you to think about *why* your tween is doing what she is doing, and to draw on the ability that already exists in you in order to accept, understand, or modify it. Often, we look to experts to tell us what to do or lay out a plan for us to follow. You are the expert on your tween. In here, you will find a broad range of topics that relate to tweens. And yes, it will cover psychological and physical development of the tween years. But more importantly, it will provide the foundation to put you in the driver's seat.

Understanding fundamental issues is important, but you know best what type of a parent you are as well as the unique personality of your tween. Think about a time when you have expressed frustration about a conflict with another person to a friend. Your friend proceeds to tell you how you should handle it, only to leave you thinking "that isn't my style at all!" Telling a quiet person to boldly confront someone won't work. Telling an overprotective parent to lighten up won't work (I can speak to this one from experience!). Likewise, me telling you one single way to parent won't work either. I want you to know your own style and be able to weave your strengths together with the information provided to create a powerful ally for your daughter.

And best of all, I do have an expert co-writing this book with me: my daughter! Kendall kept a notebook starting at age 9 which will help illustrate key differences that occur as the tween years unfold. She also lends some perspective into what is really going on with tweens. She is here to give her two cents about the topics in this book, and my advice about them. Sometimes she agrees, knowing that tweens might resist this or that, but ultimately it is important. And sometimes she wants us to know when an idea in here will likely be an uphill battle. She even has some suggestions of her own. Kendall's role in this book is to provide levity, she posts "Kendall's Corner" at the end of every chapter. She has brought some important lessons to my attention, and shown me that given the opportunity (and by 'opportunity' she means SPACE!), tween girls are very capable of making positive and mature choices.

I chose to write only about tween girls. This is simply because I feel there are enough unique aspects to the experience of being and parenting a tween girl to warrant a book of their own.

Through all of my years of school, the points and details that I remember the most are the ones that came attached to stories and examples. For me, personal stories are a wonderful way to feel connected to a person and their experience. I always enjoy them and learn from them. This is my hope for you through this book. There is, of course, essential information throughout; but I could not keep myself from peppering this book with stories and examples. I hope you receive this in the positive light that it was intended – a way for you to relate to others and experience many moments of "me too!"

Has It Always Been This Way?

You've probably heard talk show banter about tweens, or had discussions in your social circle. We often hear it reported that girls are growing up so much quicker now, and how different things are now than when we were their age. Is this really the case, or does every generation feel that they were remarkably different than the generation that follows? Well, the answer is that there is truth to both sentiments. Every generation of parents has lamented that the world was a much different place when they were growing up. Our parents all walked five miles to school, uphill – both ways, in the snow, right? But the truth is, of course things change from generation to generation. And the new generation of tweens is no exception.

Two or three decades ago, parents of girls worried primarily about drug and alcohol use, eating disorders, and sexual activity – especially with AIDS as the new concern on the scene. We still worry about these things today, but add dating violence, bullying and cyber-bullying, pedophiles, sexting, driving under the influence and distracted driving, and the seemingly endless issues created by tween safety online. Of course issues such as dating violence, pedophiles, and bullying existed in past generations, but the level of awareness and focus these topics received was nowhere near what it should have been and is today.

I do believe that there is some value in waxing nostalgic about how things used to be. The dinner conversations and chats with friends about our youth and even our parents' youth helps to clarify our values and how we hope our children experience the world. It illuminates the hopes and dreams we have for our children, as well as shedding light on the obstacles that may stand in the way of realizing these dreams. The problem with constantly looking back is that we sometimes look back with rose-colored glasses. It's easy to look back at our childhoods through adult lenses. Bullying wasn't as bad, teachers cared more, parents were more effective, etc. While it's interesting to research and compare how things *really* were decades ago, it doesn't help us parent today.

As parenting challenges come up, we naturally recall our own childhoods. Some of the information presented is backed up by stories from when I grew up. As I said, this can help us to clarify issues. It gives us the frame of reference from which we make decisions. If a classmate is being mean to your daughter, you may recall a similar incident from your childhood. In processing the events from your history, you will either realize that you or your parents handled it poorly, or that you appreciate how the issue was resolved. This allows you the opportunity to form your own plan of action based on your values. Of course, some issues are timeless – uncomfortable sex talks, being embarrassed by our parents, and kids' complaints about rules and limits.

That's how and why I wrote this book. As you are reading, my hope is that you are able to blend the relevant research or psychological information with your own experiences. You can borrow my stories, too, and use your understanding of yourself and your tween to find out where you are and where you'd like to be in terms of raising your tween.

Kendall's Corner: God made us all with strengths and weaknesses and writing is not one of my strengths, but I still hope that what I write will be meaningful and helpful to you. My mom is very entertaining and also very smart. As a psychologist she is a very good mom. Sure she gets on my nerves but what mom doesn't? She is an amazing mom and I don't know what I would do without her. I know my mom loves me because she tells me all the time, and she takes such good care of me. But she is also embarrassing! Mostly this is when she takes me out in public and is weird – which usually involves dancing.

I have learned that being a tween is harder as you get older. Moms, let your daughter be herself, she might be moody but that is because she is changing to a teen so give her some space!

Chapter 1
Puberty

I will admit to you that this was my least favorite chapter to write. I much prefer to get into the more active phases of raising a tween, the nitty gritty stuff where you are really *doing* something, not just *knowing* something. However, it makes sense to include puberty in this book because it is relevant. The medical and basic facts are important to know and are unavoidable. But I'm not a doctor, and my aim is to bolster your relationship with your tween by how you interact with her. There will, of course, be fundamental information, but I plan to impart less about *what* the information is and more about *how* to use it to reach this goal. Let's wade through the medical lingo so that you know what you need to know, and more importantly – you know how to use the information. And I promise to try and make it as entertaining as possible.

What's Going on During Puberty

Hormones

We blame a lot on hormones, right? When boys start paying attention to girls we accuse them of having 'raging hormones'. When women are moody or emotional, they are 'hormonal'. From puberty on, in fact, so much is attributed to hormones that it can become white noise. It has become one of those words that lose all meaning because we hear them so often

– like calories... or literally (or do those words just lose meaning for me!).

Anyway, it is true that most unflattering feelings, behaviors, and qualities tend to be blamed on hormones, and certainly this term is overused. But the reality is that hormones do play a role in the development of a tween. Once the contribution that hormones make in our tweens is better understood and clarified, we can recognize their function in our lives without overstating or misrepresenting every issue as a function of hormones. Great, you say, how does this make my tween stop rolling her eyes at everything I say? Well, first things first.

Estrogen production by the ovaries at the onset of puberty begins to cause changes in girls in order to transition their bodies from girls to women. Now don't start yawning yet. Much of this may be a review of what you already know, and a reminder of what us women went through ourselves perhaps decades ago. This won't be an exhaustive biological explanation of all things tween medical, but the changes in tweens' bodies cannot go unmentioned, and clarifying this information helps us explain and understand our tweens that much more. So here's what hormones begin to kick into gear:

Height

Around age 9 begins what is often referred to as an increase in growth velocity (1). This refers to the fact that in earlier childhood, growth each year was fairly slow. Puberty begins an increase in height that peaks during the adolescent growth spurt. The increase in height during puberty accounts for approximately 20% of final adult height, a total of about 9-11 inches for girls. Notably, while the increase in height begins at age 9 for girls, it begins at age 11 in boys and peaks for them at age 13 ½, while the peak is age 11 ½ for girls. If you've ever walked down the halls of a middle school, this fact is quite evident. And if you find yourself worrying that your daughter's height will continue Jack and the Beanstalk style, know that typically girls add only about two inches after they begin menstruating.

Weight

Weight gain during puberty seems much more complicated and variable. Girls will likely notice more body fat along the upper arms, thighs, and upper back, and hips tend to grow wider (2). These changes can be a difficult for some tweens. If the changes are gradual enough, some may barely notice them. Others may be glad to have a more grown up body and lose the little kid look. But others may feel awkward in their own skin. It may be difficult to fit into clothes, and they may suddenly be aware that they are bigger in one way or another than their peers. Worst of all, well-meaning friends and family may make remarks about their size.

Weight is a major factor in tween self-image. I'm sure that you can attest to the fact that the issue of weight and body image follows us into adulthood (did I say follows? I meant stalks, relentlessly pursues, and hounds!). So anything we can do to set up a healthy and positive foundation now will buffer our tweens now as well as later on. Because it's a lengthy discussion, we will talk about how to foster a positive body image in the chapter on what influences our tweens.

Back to Puberty – Hair Production and
Breast Development

While breast development is often the first sign of puberty, body and pubic hair growth may be the first sign for others. Though girls have always had hair on their arms and legs, this is the time when it may become thicker or darker. Many girls around age 9 or 10 wish to begin shaving their legs because of an increased awareness of their body hair. I don't know about you, but this seemed like a much bigger deal to our moms. It was a big deal when a girl started shaving her legs, and moms were very outspoken about things like not shaving above the knee, and warnings about how shaving makes the hair grow back with a vengeance.

Because of my memories of this time, I always had in the back of my mind that it would be a big deal when Kendall wanted to shave her legs. But actually, I didn't really think much of it. As I'm writing this, she is 12, and hasn't started shaving her legs yet. She has mentioned it one time that I recall, mostly just a "weird that girls are shaving their legs now, I wonder when I should" kind of a comment. Other than wanting to make sure she doesn't feel pressured to start before she's ready, concerns about her cutting herself (she's clumsy!), and a complaint about how expensive razors are, I'm okay with Kendall starting to shave her legs whenever she's ready. To clear things up, many moms did (and still do) believe that shaving hair makes it grow back faster, thicker, or darker. Shaving hair blunts the ends of it, making it feel coarser. But shaving does not change the growth or look of hair (3).

The development of breasts can begin around age 9 in some girls, and later in others. Girls have a wide variety of responses to this happening in themselves or their friends. Here's what happens: One girl in say, fourth grade, is developing quickly and needs – and gets – a bra. Within weeks, almost half of the remaining girls show up with bras as well, with nary a need for one. The girl who needed it is probably the least interested in having it, which is exactly how I remember it from my youth.

The first girl to get a bra in my class was horrified to have to wear it. Her mother noticed that she would look more appropriate in clothes with one on and got one for her. She hated being the only one in class to have one. Meanwhile, the rest of us began the ritual of the "we must, we must, we must increase our bust" exercises. As the weeks went on, other girls who just couldn't stand it anymore convinced their mothers to buy them a bra. Some bragged about it, wanting credit for this milestone and status symbol. Others were quietly sporting their new undergarment, satisfied with the knowledge that they had one, ready to answer 'yes' if they were ever asked. I didn't want to ask my mom for a bra, thinking she might come back with "for what?" (For the record, this reply was unlikely to have happened; my mom is actually very sweet.)

I guess I didn't pay close enough attention, though, because it wasn't until one big day when I realized I was in the minority of non-bra wearers. That day? Scoliosis screening day. I thought we all were wearing swimsuits to be checked, but that was only for the girls who – gasp – didn't have a bra to wear instead. I remember standing in line in the room where they had girls separated from boys to be checked by the nurse. One after another of my classmates was checked wearing their bras. Only myself and a few other girls had swimsuits on. I suddenly felt like a little girl among women. It wasn't long before I finally summoned the courage to ask my mom for a training bra. Years before I actually needed it, but I've already said too much.

Even in the decades-old scenario I describe, girls have different reactions to the phenomenon of breast development. The girls who develop first are not always ready to be the leaders of the pack. The girls who develop last may think of little else until their chest makes an appearance. By middle school, most girls feel like they should have a bra regardless of need, if for no other reason than modesty. This is often because this is the age where girls change for P.E. or after school sports in a locker room. So if the subject hasn't come up by then with your tween, it may be wise to have a conversation with your daughter. We'll cover the finer points of the conversation in a moment.

Menstruation

We can't talk about puberty without talking about menstruation. The first menstrual period usually begins between the ages of 10 and 15, with an average age of 12. One clue is that the first period often begins within two years after breasts begin to appear (4). Some girls may also notice some vaginal discharge for several months before the first period begins, so she may ask you about this or you may notice this while you are doing her laundry.

As moms, it can be difficult to get in the right headspace when talking about periods. Your instinct may be to tell your daughter "good luck kiddo, because by the time you're my age you will have had cramps that make you want to cry, at least one embarrassing caught-off-guard period incident, and enough moodiness to scare off a room full of linebackers." But this may not be the message that you want to send when imparting information on this milestone. You need to get back to more of a "this is exciting and a big deal" frame of mind. Remember, you set the tone for this time in her life when you have these conversations.

Your Experiences and Your Conversation Barometer

Many factors come into play when you consider talking with your tween about puberty. Some of you think this is no problem, some of you have already had this conversation, some of you just had a chill run down your spine, and some of you started to get the giggles. I will give you some guidelines and talking points for talking to your daughter about this, but there is no exact way this conversation should be had. Every mom and every daughter is different.

What Was it Like for You?

Do you remember how you talked with your mom about getting your period? And you've probably shared these stories with enough friends to know that they all had different experiences as well. I have one friend who claims to still be traumatized by the memory of her mother telling her how to use a tampon – bent knees and hand gestures, like a horrifying game of charades. One of my sisters wasn't sure how to announce the onset of her period, so she revealed it by playing a game of 'hangman.' I simply and quietly wrote 'maxi-pads' on the shopping list, hoping they would simply appear and the subject would never be brought up. Thanks to technology, a friend's daughter sent her an e-mail to let her know that she started her period. I can only imagine how many texts have been sent with this information!

How Have Other Conversations with Your Tween Gone?

How do you normally have conversations with your daughter? If you have generally been laid back in talking with you daughter, then to orchestrate a serious sit-down talk will probably freak her out. Remember, you have been thinking about your daughter reaching developmental milestones and becoming a young woman for a long time. But that doesn't mean your daughter has been planning for this. Yes, she has likely been wondering when her chest will grow and when she might start her period, and she is no doubt curious about what is happening. This does not necessarily translate into her hopes of having a potentially embarrassing conversation with you about it.

When Kendall was in the fourth grade, the girls in her class were going to be taught about menstruation. I felt like I wanted her to hear some things from me first. This was partly just because it was a big deal to me and I wanted to handle it, and partly because I thought she might be freaked out and I wanted her to go into the day with some background knowledge.

While cooking dinner together, I said "hey, remember that you have that talk with the nurse next week. I thought I'd go over what she's going to talk to you guys about real quick." Her reply to this was "oh my gosh, Katie said her mom already told her this stuff, and it's DISGUSTING." So thanks to Katie, I was already at a disadvantage. But this let me know how ready (or not) she was for this conversation, and I took my cues from that. Despite the fact that she talks a lot (seriously, the kid talks non-stop), she does not like talking about topics like puberty.

Having the Talk (or Talks)

I favor what I call 'drive-by' conversations. Avoid the temptation to have one comprehensive talk. I'm a planner, so it would be easy for me to research what I need to say and plan a big sit-down to disseminate this information in an orderly fashion. But remember what I said just two paragraphs ago? Your daughter's curiosity and need to know this information does not translate into willingness to submit to this meeting!

Gather the information you need to impart to her, and plan to parcel it out in small doses. This accomplishes two things. First, it prevents the awkward can't-end-soon-enough pressure of a big talk. And second, it sets the stage for open communication. Your tween will come to expect and accept that talks about all aspects of growing up are more than just a one-time thing. This can especially help if she has questions that you didn't anticipate. It's quite likely that she will have an embarrassing or uncomfortable question at some point during her tween years (or beyond). If she knows that topics come up every so often, she doesn't have to summon the courage to ask you something out of the blue. It will be reassuring for her to know that an opportune time to ask you her question will present itself.

Be Prepared

It would be a big mistake to think that you are prepared for a talk about different aspects of puberty just because you have experience in these areas. You'll quickly realize that you aren't sure where to start, where to end, or what exactly you want to say. Once you've decided the topic you will cover, make yourself some notes and do any research necessary on the topic. Reputable Internet sources or books can ensure that your information is correct. You don't need to create a Power Point presentation; this is just you doing some homework before you start talking to your tween. And speaking of the Internet, be aware of the possibility that she has already been exposed to misinformation via her own computer or device, or a friend's. Asking her what, if anything, she has seen about various aspects of puberty online or from friends can be a great way to kick things off. Think of it as the most indelicate ice-breaker you've ever attempted!

In the spirit of the drive-by conversation, don't plan to cover puberty from a-z in one conversation. Some things don't require much talking at all, maybe just a quick "now that you are entering puberty, you might find some hair growing in your armpits or on your private parts, ok?" This will almost surely elicit an "eww, MOM!" response, but at least you've given the heads up. Other topics, like menstruation, may need more in-depth coverage. With Kendall, I drew a quick picture of the ovaries and uterus, just for a visual, and explained what happens.

Pick Your Moment

You know your daughter, and when she is most likely to be receptive to a conversation. Perhaps she is tired and cranky when she gets home from school but mellows out once she's had some down time and a snack. Pick a time when she is the most approachable. And know that this time may pop up unexpectedly, but given that you are already prepared, this should not be a problem. You may have heard the notion that it's great to talk to kids while you are driving them around in the car. This is often true – they are a captive audience, there is no one else around, and they feel less intimidated because you aren't staring them down. However, perhaps you have a child that likes or needs face to face time and some eye contact. If this is the case, the car may not suit your needs. In this case, maybe ask her to help you cook dinner and talk then. There is enough of a distraction if necessary, but enough opportunities to stop what you are doing and look at one another.

Anticipate Questions, or the Lack of Them

As you map out what you are going to talk about, think of where the conversation may lead. Imagine you are going over what happens during menstruation. You explain how the egg and uterine lining are shed if the egg is not fertilized. How likely is your daughter to ask how an egg is fertilized? What then? If you are fine to enter that conversation as well, have your research and planning done for that. If you aren't ready to go down that road, you had better know what you plan to say.

It's also possible that your daughter will not ask any questions; either because she just wants this talk to be over, or because she really doesn't know what to ask. This is okay. Make sure she knows that if questions pop up, you'd love to hear them. Your willingness to let the subject drop furthers her confidence that these talks aren't scary. "What do mean you don't want to know what a fallopian tube is?!" will only reinforce the idea that talking with you is something to avoid.

As I mentioned, I talked to Kendall about menstruation prior to the talk at school. After the talk, I asked her to tell me what they said. Through the course of the discussion, I said something about it being helpful to keep track of when periods come, and I realized she missed the part about periods coming every 28 days. Her impression was that this only happens once. I apparently neglected to mention the reoccurring nature of periods, and assuming the school presenter said something, she missed it. Had I not made the effort to keep the conversation going after the presentation, she would have been in for quite a shock.

It was brief bullet points with Kendall, she was shifting uncomfortably the whole time, letting me know that she was not interested in a drawn out discussion. I gave her the information that she needed, and that was good enough. Once she started middle school, I asked her if the girls at school ever talked about periods. After the obligatory eye-roll, she said they sometimes did and that when that happens she "gets the heck out of there". I asked if she had any questions about anything she heard, and she said no. I didn't press her for details. I told her what to expect if she started during school, as well as some survival skills in that scenario (tie her sweater around her waist, get to the nurse, and that any female teacher would be more than equipped and willing to assist her). I also suggested that she keep a maxi-pad in her locker or backpack as a just in case, which she actually agreed to, and we moved on.

And you know what? Kendall has sporadically come to me to ask questions. They happen during the quiet moments when I'm doing dishes or folding laundry. While my instinct is to run and hug her and gush about my happiness in our relationship, I stifle my enthusiasm, nonchalantly answer her question, ask if she has any other questions and then move on. What she doesn't see is that later, I run to my husband and squeal "she DOES need me!!," which elicits an eye roll from him – she must have inherited this trait from him, right?

It wouldn't surprise me if you were thinking that the topic of puberty involves a lot more information than you imagined. I think a lot of us envision puberty and think of a couple of bullet points and that will be it. I hope I have you realizing that it *is* a lot of information, that discussing it with your daughter requires some forethought and planning, and that it is not a one-time occasion.

Finally, remember that your daughter's doctor can be an advocate regarding many of these topics. Many doctors start talking with their tween patients about periods at annual well-child visits, and some even talk to older tweens about drinking, drugs, and sex. Your daughter's doctor may ask to speak with her alone for this part of the visit. If you are curious about what the doctor's routine with tweens is, you may want to call in advance of the visit to find out what will occur. If your daughter is reluctant to speak with you, or you are hoping for some reinforcement in a particular area, you may want to let the staff know of any concerns that you have and if the doctor might incorporate this into the visit.

The Tween Brain – Not Done Cooking

I don't like to make excuses for a lot of things. I believe that finding reasons to explain behaviors and conduct that we don't like keeps us from effectively dealing with problems. When you begin to notice emotional outbursts in your tween, well-meaning friends or family will reassure you by saying that hormones make tweens crazy, or their brains aren't developed. And then you see a segment on a talk show about just this subject, and so you are convinced – my tween is normal (and crazy). The reality is there was probably a doctor or scientist on this talk show, and you didn't understand half of what he or she said. But you heard something that made you feel better, and everyone around you seems to agree, so that's that. This is exactly what I mean; this doesn't help us to maintain a healthy relationship with our tween, it just gives us permission to accept their behavior and try to white-knuckle it until they are off to college.

12

So what is my plan? I'm going to talk to you about brain development. Okay, I mostly just said that to be funny. But seriously, I'm still going to tell you about the adolescent brain. But I will do so in a most basic way, and you have to promise me that you won't just use this as an excuse to deem your tween hopeless until adulthood. Actually, if I do this right, you will have a bare-bones understanding of the brain and how this may relate to your tween's development; but you will realize that this is only one ingredient in the complex recipe that is your daughter.

When it comes to tween brain development, what's important to know is that the brain is indeed continuing to develop. Different areas of the brain are responsible for different functions and processes, everything from motor skills to emotional processes (5). As it relates to adolescence, a great deal of the current research on brain development focuses on the connectivity in the brain and the prefrontal cortex.

Neural connections in the brain are what allow information to be transmitted. The changes and development that occur during adolescence allow for these connections to become more efficient and, in part, improve the effectiveness of the transfer of information between different regions of the brain (6).

You may have heard of the term "executive functions," and these take place in the prefrontal cortex (7). Essentially, executive functions are the cognitive skills used in goal-directed behavior. These include planning, attention, organizing thoughts, considering consequences, and understanding emotions. I'm sure you find these to be in abundant supply in your tween... okay, I'm kidding of course, just making sure you're still paying attention in the midst of the biology lesson. But there is a reason that your tween may lack some ability in the executive functions; researchers are finding that the prefrontal cortex is far from mature until at least the early 20s. If you are like me, you read this information and say one of two things – bummer, or aha!

The significance of understanding tween brain development is to bear in mind that things are indeed changing up there. More efficient connections and a burgeoning ability to judge situations and make decisions will look different for every tween. Because you know your daughter best, you will recognize how substantial the differences are in her functioning and behavior. This applies to the hormonal changes occurring as well, which we will tackle next.

The degree to which hormones influence behaviors in early adolescence is frequently studied with conflicting results (8). This is why it is important not to exaggerate the role they play. However, they do still play a part. Estrogen, for example, is much maligned for provoking mood changes in adolescents. As we saw, brain development is a factor in this as well. However, estrogen has been shown to stimulate the brain's emotional center, called the limbic system. This is believed to be where mood swings originate (9).

Similarly, estrogen is believed to be responsible for allowing the genetic expression of conditions such as depression and bipolar disorder. This means that perhaps a child is pre-disposed to a certain disorder, but the expression of this disorder is 'revealed' due to the increase in this hormone. This may, in part, explain the increase in diagnoses of depression in girls during puberty (10).

There is endless research in this area, and many interesting directions this could take us. But as I said, I just wanted to get to the basics. In six months, if your tween is having difficulty with decision making, I don't want you to think "wait a minute.... let me think, is this a neural connection thing?" I also don't want you to use this as an excuse for poor behavior in your tween, thinking "well of course she lied to me; her prefrontal cortex is not complete!"

The takeaway here doesn't need to be the ability to conjure up a brain map at every problematic juncture with your tween. I want you to realize that she is a work in progress. You will also notice what is different for *her*. Notice how she is changing in relation to how she used to be. Perhaps your daughter has always been able to demonstrate a fairly planned approach to life, so maybe the only change you will see is that she is able to do it more consistently. In other words, there is not a big change from her baseline behavior to her current way of managing. Or maybe she used to be mostly easy-going and social, but is now anxious and withdrawn. This shows a significant difference, and will require you to pay close attention to these changes to determine if you should be concerned, especially given the indication that depression increases in girls during puberty.

You'll find that keeping the changes specific to your daughter in mind will allow you to remember that in spite of her resistance, your job parenting her is not done. You may feel frustrated that she seems scatter-brained, only to reflect on earlier years and realize that she has always been that way. Maybe she seems to over-react to what others say to her, and while her brain development deems this normal, you also realize that increased school expectations and scheduling are leaving her a bit overwhelmed and lacking the time and space to process these emotions. Or you may even notice differences that compel you to seek outside assistance to determine if she is having some learning difficulties or even a mental health condition. She still requires your patience, understanding, and teaching to help guide her during this evolution.

Many friends of mine have shared with me that they are able to understand the process of puberty in their tweens because the role of hormones is fairly easy to understand and because they can relate to it. These same friends also admit that while they do not understand the process and effects of brain development, they are quite willing to blindly blame it for their tween's irrational behavior or decisions. Once they understood the same information that you just read, they felt much more centered.

In the coming chapters, we'll be talking more about how to effectively communicate with your tween in everyday-life situations as well as during problematic behaviors and discipline-worthy events. The information from this chapter will serve as a backdrop for that communication. If your tween was poorly prepared for an exam and flies off the handle at you for talking to her about it, you won't dismiss it as her crazy hormones or underdeveloped brain. Instead, you will be able to reframe the event as an opportunity for you to recognize that she may lack the skills to adequately organize her time and that her hormones perhaps shortened her fuse at your upset. Again, I assure you this is not giving her a free pass. This is giving you a chance to more accurately view the situation and act accordingly.

Knowing about brain development and puberty does not excuse bad behavior from your tween, but it may help explain it. Recognizing the biology behind a mood swing instead of being mystified and frustrated by it may just boost your confidence in parenting this age group. This awareness can help center you enough to take a deep breath and proceed in a more logical and patient manner, which will benefit everyone involved. And believe me; you'll probably have many chances to practice this.

Kendall's Corner: Okay, so let's talk about puberty. Oh wait, I just remembered – I do NOT want to talk about this subject. Sure, some girls are open about it, but many girls (including me) are not. Enough said.

Chapter 2
Creating a Foundation

We've identified that our tween girls need support to navigate the world of puberty and continued brain development. And we will soon explore the reality that these girls are inundated with inappropriate, violent, or over-sexualized content from every angle. So how can we possibly buffer girls from this influence? As daunting as it sounds, it is possible. I like to think of girls at this age as swimming in the ocean. So many girls are at the surface, being tossed about by choppy waves and splashed by the water around them. If we can't take them out of the ocean, our goal then becomes teaching them to swim just below the surface. Still in the water, but less affected by the constant change and turbulence above them. They may need to come up for air, but their time in the ocean is much less chaotic.

In the coming chapters, we will talk about concepts such as tween friendships, bullying, boys, and other areas that are influencing your tween. But as with so many things, we need to start with a solid foundation. I don't want you to simply react to every new social problem, show, song, and clothing fad that comes along. I want you to be proactive, and be able to make necessary adjustments to an established base. Building a foundation begins by asking yourself a lot of questions.

What are our family values? What qualities do I want my tween to develop? What values and expectations does my tween hold for herself? This goes back to the idea of swimming just below the surface. The ability to feel centered and confident about the values and meaningful qualities that we hold for ourselves and our children allows us to not be overwhelmed by the many choices we will have to make to allow this, forbid that, or reject this. I'm quite sure that you know what is important in your family, but it may not always be on the tip of your tongue because you have not likely written it out or really made it clear.

Wasn't it the Cheshire Cat in *Alice in Wonderland* who said "if you don't know where you want to get to, then it doesn't matter which way you go?" This is actually quite profound! You may make snap decisions that seem to make sense, and maybe they do: "No way are you wearing that out of the house....," "you are SO not seeing that movie....," etc. And though they are made with safety, modesty, or morality in mind, they are still snap decisions that have no well thought-out foundation. And most of all, they are decisions that appear to your tween to come out of the blue. We need something to serve as a basis for decisions that your tween understands and is a part of.

To that end, I love the idea of having one or more visual representations of what is important to your tween that also reflects your family's values and expectations. Lately there has been a trend in mindfulness or consciousness, so this is very timely and you'll be able to find a lot of inspiration should you need it. These representations can be projects such as a vision board or even writing a mission statement.

I will admit that these are sometimes the kind of ideas that we psychologists come up with that make our clients roll their eyes. Hokey – maybe a little. Effective and important – you bet. I have heard about more and more people embracing the idea of a vision board. They remind me of the collages I made when I was younger. You can find many ideas for these online, and encourage as much creativity as you'd like. The main idea is that your tween will find pictures from magazines, newspaper stories, personal pictures, quotes, and anything else that she finds inspirational or meaningful and arranges them on a board to display. When she looks at her vision board, she is reminded of what is important to her, what qualities she admires, and what goals she would like to attain.

If your tween doesn't like the idea of a vision board, maybe a mission statement is more her style. Most companies and organizations today have a mission statement which serves to summarize the goals and values of the company. It also provides concrete words that guide future direction and actions. Similarly, individual mission statements summarize the goals and values of your tween. Creating mission statements also allows the opportunity for your tween to clarify the direction that she'd like the future to take, and actions needed to get there.

An individual mission statement can serve as the groundwork for your tween to understand herself as an individual, and begin to take ownership of and power over her circumstances. This is something that is meant to be positive and provide a frame of reference for your tween, and does not need to be a pressure-filled activity meant to sum up her entire existence. I couldn't possibly write a mission statement defining my future goals as a senior citizen, and tweens can't be expected to write one looking as far ahead as their college, adult, or even high school years. For this reason, the mission statement should focus on around the next two or three years of her life. Here are the steps and guidelines to writing a personal mission statement.

- Begin by looking at examples of mission statements. Look at companies that you know and use, or even your tween's school. This simply familiarizes your tween with the concept, and provides some inspiration.

- Come up with a list of character traits and behaviors to enhance the writing process, use a search engine to generate a comprehensive list to add to her own if you need to.

- To get her excited about it, call it whatever you'd like. Mission statement might sound too dull or grown up. Ask her to name it – Paige's Plan, Lexi's Life, Sara's Survival Guide. You get the idea. Make it something fun and relatable.

- Encourage brevity. Anything longer than four or five sentences will be hard to remember and embrace, and will start to feel like homework.

- Include both character and behaviors. What primary character traits does your tween admire and hope to develop further? What behaviors support these characteristics and have the most positive impact at this time in her life?

- Avoid saying what she won't do, focus on what she can and will in order to keep it positive. For example, instead of saying "I don't want to have bad friends," she could say "I will work on having positive friendships."

- Her mission statement should provide direction for daily activities and decisions. Writing "I will be ready to be a responsible teenager" is a great goal, but this statement does little to direct day-to-day actions and to focus on now. Ensure that her mission statement can be a part of her daily life.

- If you feel your tween would do better with some guidelines rather than a blank page, provide a template.

This allows her to plug in her values and goals without veering off course. Try one of these, or create your own:

- "It is important to me to be/become/be more ... (insert two or three character traits) because (say why this is significant). I will (insert one or two specific behaviors or actions that will support the character traits) so that (what will the feeling or reward for doing this be)."

- "I admire (insert two or three character traits). In order to develop these traits in myself, I will (insert one or two specific behaviors or actions that will support the character traits) during all parts of my life. I will know that I am succeeding when (insert signs that will signal progress)."

Remember that a mission statement is not cast in stone. It will continue to change and evolve as your tween gains insights about herself and what she wants out of each part of her life. She shouldn't need to change it weekly, but once a year or so is acceptable.

If you are really fond of this idea, you may wish to have other family members create mission statements as well. Beyond this, consider making a family mission statement. This is a great way to open up a discussion about what you stand for as family, and serves as a great base from which decisions are made and understood. Talking about what values your family cares about as well as why provides a broader view of your family's place in your community and the world.

Whether she has created a vision board, mission statement, or other representation, find a clever way to display it. Post it on a display wall, put it on the refrigerator, or frame and embellish it. When situations arise, refer to it. My disclaimer is that you need to avoid using this as a weapon. If she irritates you by hounding you for sweets before dinner instead of cleaning her room, I don't recommend saying "your mission statement says you're supposed to be more helpful at home, maybe you should go re-read that part!" More likely, she may bring up a problem she is having with friends, and instead of telling her for the tenth time that she needs to be nice, you can say "I know you are working on treating people as you wish to be treated, how does what happened today fit into that?" This prevents her from thinking you are lecturing her again, and begins to let her take ownership of her actions.

Take each situation as it comes. Some situations may not require any mention of her vision board or mission statement at all, while others might benefit from actually looking at it or reading over what she wrote and talking about how these apply to the situation. If she wrote that she would like to be more respectful or has a picture on her board of being the class valedictorian but had a run in that day with a teacher, this is a great tool to work through the issue. Ask her where she fell short of her goal and what she needs to do about it. She likely has ideas all on her own. Maybe she needs to keep a stress ball in her hands during class to squeeze when she feels frustrations rising with her teacher. Maybe she feels that she should write an apology to the teacher. Again, this begins to turn the tide from you telling her what she did wrong and what to do about it to you simply facilitating a discussion that leads to her solving her own problem – using her own words or ideas. This is so empowering for her, and minimizes tension between the two of you.

I love my mission statements, and have seen some really neat vision boards, but I realize this just may not resonate with you or your tween. Please don't give up the concept entirely. Find something to use, even if it's just finding a motivational saying that she likes and either typing and framing it or perhaps using some vinyl stickers to put up on her wall. Kids with media devices are quite fond of electronic wallpaper that they find online with inspirational sayings, ask her to find one that really speaks to her and serves the same purpose as the other ideas. It is certainly not the be all and end all of tween parenting. But I promise it will help set the stage and continue the development of her value system, character, goal-setting ability, and accountability.

Kendall's Corner: I made a mission statement and honestly, I thought it was going to be stupid until I started writing it. My mom is always coming up with things like this, and there is no point trying to get out of it. But then I realized I sort of liked it, I never thought about what my goals are. I have even been thinking about it when I need to make a decision, it can help me make the right decision. And I like that my mom doesn't ask me about it or talk about it all the time, just once in a while she'll ask me how something fits in with my mission statement, or how a decision I'm making might be easier if I remember my mission statement. Here's my mission statement:

> I, Kendall Racanelli, want to be everything God wants me to be including a good Catholic person. I want to be funny, smart, nice, and fantabulous while still being a good person and student.

(Note from mom: notice that Kendall's statement doesn't totally fit the criteria I laid out, she didn't include the behaviors that she will exhibit to live this out. I still included it here to show you that it is good enough. She started out by only saying she wanted to be 'fantabulous,' so I did ask her to expand this to include other, more specific, character traits. It was more important for her to feel some pride and ownership in her statement than for me to correct her and ask her to change it again. I point this out so you, too, will avoid the temptation to grade and correct your daughter's work – if she put thought into it and it's meaningful, it's fine.)

Chapter 3
A Look at What
Influences Your Tween

This is the time when young girls begin to place greater importance on what their friends and peers are doing, and begin to assert their independence from parents. (Grab a tissue, dab your eyes, and read on). This process is normal and even healthy; and besides, even if we wanted to, we couldn't stop it! In no way does this mean that you are irrelevant in your tween's life. Your guidance, support, and love are crucial and despite her eye rolling, she *will* hear you. It's no wonder that girls want to act older than they are, though, as this is what they are seeing and reading about.

Clothes

It can almost sneak up on you. Clothes for your daughter used to seem so easy when she was younger, maybe she didn't even mind if you picked them out for her. But suddenly you go clothes shopping for your tween (or even younger), and you will see not just tank tops, but tank tops with lace trim. You'll see the length of shorts and skirts become alarmingly short. And my favorite, you'll see brand names or words like 'sassy', 'fun', or 'sporty' in bold letters across the butt.

Clothes are a big deal for kids. The early tweens are focused on not appearing 'babyish', it's important to them to show that they are aware of trends and brand name clothing.

26

Older tweens maintain the focus on brand names and trends, and are also interested in looking more like teenagers. Their focus may shift from the clothes themselves to how they look *in* them. All tweens may comment about how they look fat, thin, tall, short, or 'dorky' in certain clothing items, but this is much more common as tweens approach the 12 year old mark. It makes sense – when they are younger, they start to think about the Hello Kitty on their shirt. As they get older, they think about how the Hello Kitty shirt makes them look. Then they near middle age and wonder if Hello Kitty can cover up a muffin top, but that's another book!

The way you handle selecting clothes can set the tone for many other decisions. Don't enter a shopping trip bracing yourself for a battle, enter with a positive attitude and belief that this is an opportunity to empower her while setting appropriate limits. Here are some do's and don'ts to help you survive the clothing store.

Do plan ahead. If you are in need of specific items, make a list of what you need. If you are okay buying a few splurge or impulse items, give both you and her an idea of how many you might allow. Many departments intended for tweens are chalk full of items that are irresistible to them, and it can be overwhelming to sort through items and try to stop the barrage of "OMG – I *have* to have this!" Head this off by going over the list with her. "We are looking for two pairs of jeans, two or three fall shirts, and a new pair of dress shoes. I will consider no more than two other items if we find something really cute, but we only have $200 to spend today." And if the toddler years taught you nothing else, I hope that you are consistent and follow through with what you say. If your tween knows you are a pushover, this plan may quickly unravel. More on consistency later, back to shopping...

Do let your tween know that you value her opinion. "I love your fashion sense and the things you pick out. I want you to get things that you love, but I want to make sure they are appropriate, ok? So let's get lots of options and we can narrow them down together." I prefer this to "don't drive me crazy in here, and if something's trashy, don't even think about trying to get me to buy it." And by the way, I have actually heard several different versions of this comment throughout many a shopping trip; I'll bet you have, too!

Don't go if you don't have time to negotiate with your tween. If you are in a rush and think you'll just pop in and out of the store, you are probably setting yourself and your tween up for frustration. Too little time to shop means that you won't be able to express concern over one outfit with enough time to find a suitable alternative. I'm not suggesting you make a shopping trip take hours, I'm sure time is a hot commodity in your household. I'm simply suggesting that you gauge your time and make sure you won't be in a hurry, because your need to leave quickly will make you more likely to either give in to something you don't want her to buy, or to snap and leave your tween feeling powerless.

Do be willing to compromise and be creative. Maybe you think the "v" in that v-neck is too deep but your tween loves the shirt. Would wearing a tank top underneath be an option? Or if you feel like the material or shape/size of that skirt isn't substantial enough – how about leggings underneath? You get the idea – working on a compromise about an item of clothing lets your tween know that you are trying to work with her and let her wear what she wants. And it also increases the chances of being able to say yes more often which creates a positive outlook on future outings. Kendall is a big fan of the 'throw a tank top underneath it' approach, and this has become a staple in her wardrobe. She doesn't like leggings, but because she's seen the efforts at creative solutions to clothing issues, she knows that skirts not up to snuff are just going to have to go back on the rack and there is likely something equally awesome around the corner.

Do be aware of her school's dress code or modesty guidelines – and don't be afraid to enlist them as allies during negotiations. Not every school has a specific dress code, but almost every school lists expectations for dress in the student handbook. Be aware of what is allowed, perhaps tank tops require a 3-finger width, for example. Of course you want to comply with school guidelines, so it is okay to point out to your tween that something she likes is simply not on the approved list at school.

I can almost guarantee that you will receive the comeback that no one follows those rules and the school does little to enforce them (except in extreme cases). This may very well be true, I know this is the case for many friends I've spoken to. Respond with something like "I know lots of girls don't follow those rules, but that doesn't make it okay for you. I'd hate to see you be the one they decide to make an example out of. I understand that you like this shirt, but I'm not comfortable with you breaking the rules and I think it's too revealing as well. If you like this color I saw some similar shirts over there, let's keep looking." Then remember the original proclamation – "I really want you to find something you like, but I need to be okay with it, too." Shop. Discuss. Repeat. You'll get there!

Television and Movies

The subject matter that tweens are subjected to in television and movies is shocking. Even if you don't let your tween watch some of these shows or movies, I'll bet you have been surprised at the graphic nature of the commercials for them. I have to admit, television and movies have been the biggest source of stress for me as a parent to a tween. To me, they are the most pervasive and invasive forms of media out there.

I am possibly part of the problem. There, I said it. Or perhaps I am more like collateral damage. Here's the thing – I like television. We actually don't watch all that much television, but we have some favorite shows and we like to watch maybe an hour to decompress before bed. Most of my friends and family would tell you that I am more restrictive of the shows that Kendall can see than a lot of people. I feel like I am middle of the road. Many of Kendall's friends watch crime scene dramas and similar shows, or will talk about seeing an episode of The *Real Housewives* with their mother. Kendall does not see anything like this. The sad thing is I can't even say that keeping her from these mature shows has kept inappropriate content from coming into our living room – far from it. I was afraid I was going to have to field some tough questions after seeing the Viagra commercials during a football game.

I'm not going by industry ratings here, but we select shows that we think of as family shows, and are caught off guard far too often. Watching *Dance Moms* uncovers a barrage of profanity and talk of affairs, and we've noticed talk of use or overuse of alcohol on almost every sitcom from *Modern Family* to *Last Man Standing* (sometimes there is a lesson at the end, but it still catches us off guard). And don't even get me started on the questions brought up about diet and teen moms after seeing *Here Comes Honey Boo Boo*. We like to watch *America's Got Talent*, but more than once my husband and I have lunged for the remote when someone comes on doing a stripper pole dance.

We, like millions of other families, enjoyed rooting for contestants on different singing competition shows. I was always uncomfortable watching these shows, but I could never quite put my finger on why. And then I realized that during the initial auditions, the way that contestants were talked to, humiliated, and laughed at was disgusting and not something I wanted Kendall to see. I was haunted by the thought that no one seemed to recognize that these were real people who had to go home and relive the humiliation once the show aired. This parallels what often happens in schools. Kids are made fun of and ridiculed, but the humiliation doesn't end once the halls are emptied. These kids have to go home and either tell their parents what happened, or quietly suffer the memory of their awful day. And if the humiliation finds its way into cyberbullying, that's a whole different story. We'll talk about bullying later, but this example underscores that what kids see on television is all too often echoed in their lives. A show that features the demeaning of a person, and even promotes it in previews of the show, can influence and desensitize tweens. Television and real life don't exist separately.

Tweens and Weight

Now, in writing about how to talk to your tween about the changes in her body shape, I must gently suggest that you've already screwed up. Trust me, I would love to sugar coat this for you, but I wouldn't be doing you any favors. I wouldn't tell you this if there was no hope to make this right. I'm sure you are not surprised when I tell you that we live in a society that is critical of less than ideal (read: impossible) body sizes and obsessed with outward appearance.

It will also not surprise you when I tell you that my peers in the world of psychology have spent many years and a great deal of effort on studies that all essentially tell us one thing – the obsession with superficial and unrealistic appearance is bad. One such study found that almost 70 percent of girls aged 13-19 surveyed had a celebrity idol, and have attempted to or would like to look like this person (11). Sadly, this didn't exactly surprise me. Something that did leave me discouraged was research that showed that more than 80 percent of girls had tried dieting at least once by age 10 (12). Age 10! At Kendall's school, there was a group of girls in fifth or sixth grade that prided themselves on eating only salads at lunch. They wanted their classmates to know that this was their 'thing', and that their goal was to 'not get fat.'

Through the depressing studies, I did find a ray of hope that should catch your attention. While one study found that being exposed through media and advertising to idealized body images lowers body image satisfaction in young adult females (13), another study refined this notion a bit. This study found that for pre-adolescent and adolescent girls, the exposure to idealized body images increased the tendency to compare themselves to the ideal, but did not lower their self-perception of physical attractiveness (14).

What these studies show, then, is that our tweens are so frequently exposed to super thin and celebrity-type images that they begin to compare themselves to this ideal. They think this is what you have to look like to be happy, popular, and successful. The silver lining, however, is that this likely means the negative body image that is often created tends to come later. Although they are already being indoctrinated to think this way, they are still young enough not to hate their own bodies yet. Perhaps they still possess the 'when I grow up' mentality that delays negative body image. They are thinking this is what they will look like in 2... 5... 10 years, it hasn't occurred to them that they should look like this now. At least not their actual body, it is possible that for a time they are pacified by the external items that imitate their idol – clothes, cosmetics, and media. This tells me that increasing or maintaining a positive body image in our tweens is not a lost cause. Let's keep talking to further explore the things we should do and not do.

Have you been guilty of talking about dieting or complaining about any aspect of your body in front of your daughter? It's pretty hard not to. Even if you made an effort to not speak poorly about your body in front of your daughter, maybe someone offered you a piece of cake and instead of saying "no thank you," you said "oh my gosh, if I have that I will never fit into these jeans again" or "I'd have to work out for a week." Each of these instances sticks with our daughters.

I did make a conscious decision to never complain about my body in front of Kendall. I remember a few times getting dressed to go somewhere and thinking "wow, these jeans buttoned yesterday, right?" But instead of shaking a fist to the heavens, I would smile at her and say "well I am ready to get out there!" I think I did a pretty good job, but I am quite sure that I made self-deprecating remarks in front of other people, just like the example. It's one thing to not make comments out loud while at home, it's another to act pleased with your body and looks to other people. We just aren't supposed to do that. If a friend compliments our looks, we aren't supposed to say "thanks, I thought I looked nice, too!" We are supposed to say something like "well thank goodness for Spanx, right?"

Where does this leave us? With a need to self-evaluate. It's frustrating to realize that the world we live in is superficial, unrealistic about body size, and critical. There's not much we can do about that. It's a worthy goal to want to shift these harmful cultural trends, but that's a topic for another book. Right now I want to focus on not being a part of the problem and supporting healthy body image in our girls.

Making it Better – Watch What You Say

Take a good, hard look at what you say to or around your daughter. About you and your weight/shape, your friends and family, hers, her friends, celebrities. You get the idea. Have you spoken judgmentally about people? Being honest about your views on weight issues can be difficult, and there is so much at play here. If you have struggled with weight issues, you may have been hyper-aware of diet and exercise because you wanted to spare your daughter this struggle.

Or maybe you have been mostly aware of the need to keep critical comments to a minimum, but have let a few disparaging comments fly, just to play the socially acceptable game of not appearing to sing your own praises. Once you recognize the impact that this has on your daughter, the part you play is huge. First order of business – stop doing this. Luckily, this is one of the easier tasks to complete. Once you realize how much or how little you have made comments over the years, you can't un-know this. You will catch yourself the next time you are tempted to say something with very little effort.

Watch What You Watch

We are a bit obsessed with the show *The Biggest Loser* in our home. Besides rooting for the contestants and witnessing their journeys, it gives Kendall (and us) a break from watching the stick thin world on so many other shows. The focus on this show is health – you'll see very little attention paid to appearance and much attention paid to living a healthy lifestyle. Once a contestant is voted off, they show a follow up at the end of the show, updating how that contestant is doing weeks or months after leaving the show. They are generally still in the process of losing weight, but are much closer to the size of the average (non-obese) American. I love that we have the opportunity each time to say "wow, how awesome is that, they look so happy," or "I love that she's so healthy and doesn't have the back problems anymore." Compare this to watching a model search show, where girls who are 5' 10" and 102 pounds get into cat fights with one another after splitting a stick of gum and a diet Coke for dinner.

Avoiding programs that are extremely superficial and provide no positive role models is a start. Any of the *Real Housewives* come to mind (shameless admission – I love these shows, but don't watch them with Kendall, they are safely hidden away on the DVR until she goes to bed). Look for opportunities to model healthy values in any shows that you watch. Instead of commenting on how much weight an actress has put on or lost, or commenting on looks at all, find other things to talk about. The ways that people or characters relate to each other, the intelligent way in which they speak, healthy foods they eat, the way they look at problems, etc. It may take a little practice, but once you get the hang of it you'll find there are so many other things to talk about in shows and movies than just how the characters look. Of course if there is a character that is an average size, not unrealistically thin, I think it's great to compliment that. You just don't find much of that on television or movies!

Music

I remember when I was in high school in the late 1980s. One of my twin sisters asked for the Salt N Pepa album for Christmas, which my mother innocently purchased for her. All was jolly until my sister excitedly put the record on and played the song "Push It." Remember that one? Yikes. My dad yelled for the better part of Christmas morning. He also did some yelling when he saw the cover of the Twisted Sister album where Dee Snider is in a weird leather outfit, crazy long hair and makeup, holding that giant turkey leg, but I digress. The point of this is that, yes, there were racy lyrics all those years ago that parents did not find appropriate for their kids. And songs like "Push It" were hardly subtle. But the increase in overt and vulgar language in songs is alarming.

And yet, we sometimes miss the message in these songs, either because we haven't paid attention or because it takes a while to decipher the lyrics in difficult to understand songs. But guess what? Our tweens know the words. Have you ever been driving somewhere while listening to the radio with little ones in the car, and heard them start singing the words? And then been horrified at the words they are singing? I hate to admit it, but this has happened a few times too many to me. First, I think what a peppy song this is, then I wonder how Kendall knows the words, and quickly I stifle a scream while changing the station because I realize she now knows the word 'ho'.

I have been known to ban many a song. Kendall's dad is on board with avoiding sleazy music, but I know that when he is singing along to a song on the radio he generally sings the wrong words anyway, so I don't rely on his judgment in this area. He often reports driving Kendall home from somewhere and describing the process of finding a song that they like on the radio only to be reminded by Kendall that she's not allowed to listen to it. This is great... for now. I know a couple of things to be true. First, she will quickly get tired of having so many songs be off-limits to her when many of her friends have no such restrictions. And second, as she gets older, she will not be so willing to admit to her dad or others that she is not allowed to listen to a song. In other words, this is a short-term solution.

Awareness is the key to minimizing exposure to inappropriate music. Know what music your tween likes and what the lyrics are. In the car, do your best to listen to stations less likely to play offensive music and not even have the other stations as a pre-set. Or if your car has the option of playing from your iPod or other device, have these gadgets pre-loaded with approved music. In other words, the best offense is a good defense. If an offending song happens to find its way into your car or elsewhere, it's fine sometimes to say that you have a problem with that song and would like to change the station. It's also fine to just find a distraction; say "oh, I forgot to tell you the funniest story..." and turn down the music to tell it.

Books

I have admittedly always been fussy about the books that I read to Kendall or that she was allowed to read. I stopped reading certain series with her because the main characters were so sassy and oppositional, I didn't want Kendall getting any ideas! This, of course, was an overreaction on my part. The books were perfectly fine and characters' behavior could be used as a talking point. But I discovered a troubling inconsistency when Kendall was around sixth grade. She was required to read books, but the books available at this grade level were unacceptable to me. When she was 10 and 11, the books at this reading level were often about high school. Many girls in Kendall's classes were reading the *Twilight* and *Hunger Games* series. This is much different than just a sassy character in the earlier series. I loved these books, but I am just not okay with the sexual overtones and overt violence in certain books for Kendall.

My biggest advice in the area of books is to not assume that a book marketed toward this age group or grade level is appropriate. If you have time to read it ahead of your tween, that's great. The reality is that many of us don't have this time, especially if you have more than one child that you are previewing books for. At the very least, flip through the pages, you'll get an idea of the theme and the language used in the book.

Book store and library staff can be very helpful if you let them. Don't just tell them you are looking for a book for a tween, let them know your daughter's age. And most importantly, let them know you are concerned about inappropriate language or themes in the books. Ask them for books that don't have what you don't want – sexual themes, drug or alcohol use, or any other areas you would like to avoid. They can help weed out books with more mature themes and language. Your tween's teachers and/or school library staff can also be invaluable. Check in with them about books that they recommend, and mention the concern for inappropriate content to them as well.

Once you have settled on a book list for your tween, make sure to check in with her about the book. No need to request a formal summary, just casually ask questions about what she is reading. What's the main character like? Who do you most relate to in this story? Could you see this story happening here? How do the characters treat each other? Find some talking points about the story to not only gauge the storyline, but also to reveal any opportunities for further discussion. Perhaps your daughter will say that the characters in the book are friends, but they are much nicer to each other than her friends are to each other. What a golden opportunity to find out more about that.

I realize it sounds like it will be a part-time job to find appropriate reading material for your tween. I promise, once you get started and get in the habit of doing a little digging ahead of time, you'll become very comfortable with the process. And finding ways to ask questions about her book without sounding overbearing may feel unnatural at first, but using the above examples or coming up with your own open-ended questions will soon be second nature.

Video Games

This topic is fodder for many talk shows and water-cooler discussions. And every time there is a tragic, violent incident, this topic is brought up. For our purposes, I will keep the discussion relevant and focused. Among tweens, there is generally less interest in video games by girls than boys, and the games that girls do like to play tend to be less violent (15). Girls often prefer less competitive and less violent forms of games, ones that contain more social interaction. Of course there are exceptions to every rule; certainly there are girls who play violent video games. And even if girls are not seeking out these games, they can be exposed to them through friends or siblings. If for no other reason than awareness, you should know what games are out there and the possible effects they are having on our culture.

Poring over research in this area, it becomes apparent that there are many different ways that researchers approach this topic. And it is easy to conclude a review of the literature with more questions than answers. The psychologist in me is fighting the urge to delve too deeply into this subject, there are entire books written on the subject. But I promised you I would not lose focus, so I will present the nuts and bolts of what I believe to be true about video games.

There is continued debate over the extent to which violent video games contribute to violent behavior. One study that represents versions of many others is a study in which some students were asked to play a violent video game and others were asked to play a non-violent video game. Players were asked to 'punish' their opponents with noise blasts after playing. Those who had played the violent game punished their opponents for a longer period of time than the students who had played the non-violent game (16). Studies such as this play out in different ways in countless research papers. Other studies look for correlations between game playing habits, aggressive behavior, disciplinary problems, and academic achievement.

In my opinion, it does not matter where you fall in this debate. At best, these games do not contribute to aggressive or violent behavior as significantly as many believe. But the worst-case scenario is that, indeed, these games impact our youth in a very negative way. I believe that violent video games may be more harmful than watching violent television or movies because they are interactive, more absorbing, and may allow the player to identify with the villain in the game. In sum, there's not much of an upside here. Do your best to limit exposure to violent video games by not purchasing them for your home, and by asking the parents of your tween's friends about the use of these games in their homes.

The American Academy of Pediatrics recommends that this age group spend no more than one or two hours with entertainment media per day – this includes television, movies, and computer time as well as video games (17). Set these limits for your tween, and explain to her why you do not want her to play these video games or watch others playing them. If she really enjoys video games, work together to find ones you can both agree on, and continue to set limits on the time spent playing them. Following this advice will prevent your tween from spending too much time engaged in video gaming, even if violent games find their way into her world. Encourage her to spend time in outdoor play, hobbies, reading quality books, or interacting with family or friends.

Peers

The above categories all seem to culminate in or be reinforced by peer influence. Remember when your darling little girl wore what you picked out (or at least chose from what you bought) and liked what you liked? I remember Kendall studying how I ate or laughed or stood in an attempt to do those things just like me. Now she pays serious attention to what girls are wearing, on television and also the girls at school and on her sports teams. I'm sure you realize that this has gone on for a while; peer influence is not new to the tween scene. Kendall adored Dora the Explorer in the early years of elementary school, but I can vividly remember the day that with one swift barrage of comments from classmates, Dora was dead to her. I think she still secretly wished that she had a monkey in boots following her around on adventures, but she certainly internalized that to survive elementary school, because she needed to earn peer acceptance.

The difference between then and now is that allowing peer influence to dictate when a favorite show is too 'babyish' is one thing, and the peer influence that enters during the tween years can be quite another.

I hope you are starting to see that you have the skills necessary to plot a course through the factors that influence your tween. There are so many trends influencing your tween, but also so many ways that you are able to make an impact and a difference to buffer her from the negativity that can come from them. And while these are the primary areas that affect our tweens, there is much more to it. I've pointed out the reality that peer influence during this age becomes much stronger, but how you deal with peer issues and how you encourage your tween to navigate these issues requires much more attention. Additionally, social media is another area that warrants coverage in much greater depth. Both of these issues receive additional attention in upcoming chapters.

Kendall's Corner: At the end of the book, you'll see a 'my perfect day' writing assignment that I did for this book. It was funny to my mom and me because it covered so much from this chapter. My friends are very important to me, I want the newest technology to play my music, and I just want to do what I want to do! Of course I know this day is not really possible, but it was fun to think about.

Sometimes I do wish my mom would let me buy whatever clothes I want. Seriously, she drives me crazy. All of the shorts I pick out always seem to be "too short" or "too tight". I also don't understand the music thing. I don't see the big deal with listening to a song with a bad word in it. It's not like I don't hear those words every day, I won't mention who says them (hint – it's not my mom)! So I guess what you should take from me on these issues is that your daughter probably won't get why you have rules about these things. I can usually predict what my mom will say about clothes, music, or shows, but I don't have to like it!

Chapter 4
Friends – Part I (They Definitely Need More Than One Chapter)

I don't know about you, but I'm exhausted just thinking about all of the areas that we navigate with our tweens. No one wants to put the kibosh on everything that our daughters want, and it's made more difficult when it seems that every other tween is allowed to do whatever they like (just ask your daughter, she's the only one with limits, right?). Typically, the driving force behind most of these desires, and the people with whom your daughter will commiserate or celebrate the battle of all things trendy are friends. Friends are becoming extremely important in your daughter's life, and it is very important to nurture these relationships. Though silly or drama-filled at times, tween friendships can deeply enrich your daughter's life, bring her great happiness, teach her many life lessons, and set the stage for all of her current and future relationships. No pressure here, right!

Ever since she was little, Kendall wanted me around. She loved that I could volunteer in her classroom and chaperone field trips. She begged me to be her Girl Scout troop leader, and would not consider taking swimming lessons, ballet, or any other activity unless I was there to watch her the entire time. It was fairly easy for me to steer her away from kids that I didn't want her to play with, I simply talked up the kids I did like and set up play dates with them. If a girl in her class did something mean to her, I could say "well that's not what a friend would do, is it?" and Kendall would whole-heartedly agree and focus on the nicer girls. Of course, it was not always as cut-and-dried as this, but this was the basic scenario. Because I was in charge of her time and plans, I could guide and influence her friendships to some extent. And while she certainly had an independent streak, she generally shared my opinions. In other words, she primarily identified with me.

Just like clockwork, this began to change around age 9. I specifically remember her coming home upset about how a friend had treated her. She said "Amber ditched me at recess, I hate her." I reminded her that "we do not hate people, we can dislike what they do," to which she thought a second and then responded "nope, I'm pretty sure I hate her." Opinions like this were often backed up by other friends' opinions. And so it began – the shift to her having and proclaiming more of her own opinions and wanting more independence. I was slowly being edged out.

This is completely normal. And you know what else? It completely stinks! This was the child who wanted to know which presidential candidate I liked so that she could 'vote' for him in the mock election held by her school, who thought it was fantastic when someone mistook her for me when she answered the phone, who asked for matching Halloween costumes so we could be twins. Ahhh... those were the days.

Luckily, this does not happen overnight. You will have some time to adjust to this milestone and adapt. Of course, all girls are different, so while some girls lean pretty far into the influence of peers, some may more slowly allow this influence while still being the girl that you recognize. Kendall falls somewhere in the middle. More than once she came from a friend's house or a get-together with friends needing to be de-programmed. I'm sure you can relate. Some of Kendall's friends are allowed to speak in a more, shall we say, sassy tone (translation – these friends are rude and almost mean when speaking to their parents and seem to experience little or no consequences). So after being with this girl or girls, Kendall would come home and sort of 'try on' this tone with me. I quickly let her know that it must seem fun to be able to speak this way, but I remind her that this is not an acceptable tone in our home. Sometimes the previous sentence is what I actually say. But admittedly, sometimes I actually have more of a "who do you think you're talking to" approach. Either way, this generally resolves with some consistent reinforcement of how we speak to one another in our family.

The best example of how the importance of peers intersects with the dependence on parental support occurred when Kendall was about ten. She had been telling me about a couple of her friends that were not getting along and were putting her in the middle. I explained how this could backfire – what if one friend tells Kendall how annoying the other friend is, and that Kendall could possibly agree out of what she thinks is mindless courtesy. Well, you know what would happen next in this illustration (even as adults!)... these two friends reconcile and then one tells the other "you know, Kendall said you were annoying!" I suggested that if this scenario presents itself, Kendall should avoid answering by changing the subject or just saying "I hope you guys can be friends again." Only a couple of weeks later, I was so happy to realize that I had actually been heard. Kendall came home and said "at recess, Ashley said 'I can't stand how mean Madison is, can you?'" Excitedly, I asked Kendall how she responded. She said "I put my hand out and told her 'whoa, my mom said I am NOT supposed to answer questions like *that*.'" Once the rejoicing choir of angels settled down, I was able to appreciate that she really did listen to me – maybe not all the time, but enough to keep talking. I also realized that this was a narrow window, because I don't imagine her going with the "my mom said...." explanation when she's a teenager.

Younger tweens delight in their friendships, and often find it important to identify someone as a best friend. But during these young tween years, friendships are a lot more fluid. There may be some cliques forming or formed, but most girls are still comfortable 'floating' around different girls or groups of girls. The result is that the title of best friend can be held by many different girls, and may sometimes overlap!

Despite my knowledge of this developmental stage, I have to admit that the inconsistency in friends made me anxious. It seemed so fickle to me, and I had this nagging fear that this stage would not end and Kendall would never develop any meaningful friendships. But these types of transient friendships are quite normal and appropriate for this age. Young tween friendships are often formed and modified based on common interests, which is why they can change so often. Kendall found many new friends because they were interested in softball or shared her affinity for peace signs.

For these younger tweens, this is a time to begin to deepen their identity formation through friendships. They are seeing what they have in common with other girls, how they are alike and different from their peers, and what it means to have and to be a friend.

Older tweens tend to become more self-conscious, and begin to see themselves more as others see them (or as they *think* others see them). This begins to erode the fancy-free nature of friendships of the earlier tweens. These girls often feel that they are always on display and that their every move is being scrutinized by those around them. Because they are relatively new to this heightened sensitivity, they may misinterpret even the slightest gesture as criticism, which can be terribly upsetting to them.

I remember Kendall having a terrible day as the result of a lunchroom snub. Her school, like many others, has a peanut-free table, which is a table where kids with peanut allergies and those with lunches not containing peanuts can sit. More often than not, Kendall has some form of peanut butter or a peanut-containing granola bar in her lunch. She believed that her friend Stella knew this, and purposely conspired with another girl to bring peanut-free lunches to school to sit at this table and exclude Kendall. She came home devastated that day, and I felt so badly for her. I don't actually know whether Stella concocted this scheme to leave Kendall out, or if she and the other girl just happened to bring peanut-free lunches that day and didn't see the harm in the seating arrangement for the day. There were countless stories similar to this, and I am quite sure that you can or will be able to conjure up countless stories of the offenses committed against your tween.

This can be such a difficult time, when our tweens are off and running with their own ideas about friends and friendship. The most important thing to know is that regardless of how they are formed or changed, friends are extremely important to tweens. When you bring up questions or concerns about girls in her class, they can be met with eye rolls. It may start to feel that she no longer wants or needs your input. But whether younger or older, you can do a lot to support your tween regarding friendship issues.

Be Her Mom, Not Her Friend

I am not stirring up the debate over being friends with your kids or not. What I am saying is that when it comes to navigating tween friendships your daughter doesn't need another friend; she needs the perspective and safety of her mom. I have been in social settings of moms and daughters, and observed how some moms have responded to their daughters' comments about other girls. For example, I picked Kendall up from a birthday party, so there were four or five girls still there and a few of us moms there who showed up around the same time to pick up our daughters. It turned into something of a group discussion as the girls started to rattle off the things they did at the party and what they talked about. One of the girls told her mom "Lexi (birthday girl) told me that Abby (girl not invited to party) told her at school that she thinks my clothes are lame." I turned my attention to the mom to see how she would respond, and was shocked to hear her respond "I've seen Abby wear the same two pairs of pants all year, so I don't think we should take fashion advice from someone who doesn't even seem to own many clothes." After picking my jaw up off the floor, I remember thinking that this was the type of response I would have expected from another tween, not from a parent.

The truth is that when our daughters tell us about a girl who was mean to them, we may naturally go into protective mode, and sometimes that does not look nice. I must admit that I have had less than maternal thoughts about girls who have said something nasty to Kendall, and if I know unflattering information about the parents, this can be magnified because I may not be fond of this family to begin with. The trick is learning to keep your knee-jerk response to yourself, and then say your logical response out loud. It's quite a skill! I'm sure you have used this skill with your boss, mother-in-law, or other moms, right? Remember that your job is not to teach your daughter to be spiteful and petty, but to model for her how to get out of the grudge matches and stay on the high road.

You may feel like you are helping her by reminding her that everyone has flaws and that these other kids are not better than your daughter. But keep in mind that her day is filled with girls who will offer a snappy retort or ideas to get back at the girls who offended her. If the girl from the birthday party went back to school and told her friends what Abby had said about her clothes, you can bet that most of the girls said nasty things about Abby and began to pick apart Abby's wardrobe and personality. The last thing she needs is to go home and hear her mom doing the same. Bottom line – she knows plenty of other tweens, but she only has one mom.

Be a Good Listener, but Know When You Need to Speak Up

Instead of going on the attack when your daughter tells you about a friend or classmate who said or did something mean, acknowledge (to yourself) your anger that someone hurt your baby and then try doing more listening than talking – at least initially. Toward the end of fifth grade, Kendall started having a problem with her friend Sarah. From the time they met, Sarah was very possessive of Kendall. Her teacher even contacted me to let me know that when the class would gather on the floor at the front of the classroom for group time, Sarah would scout out a spot and shoo kids away from the spot next to her, declaring the spot for Kendall (and demanding that Kendall sit there). She tended to try to isolate Kendall from other girls and keep her all to herself. Halfway through the year, Morgan was a new student in the class, and Sarah began to be friends with her as well.

By the end of the year, something started to happen as the class would head to the cafeteria for lunch and then recess. As they walked outside, Sarah started telling Kendall "me and Morgan are playing by ourselves today, I'll think about letting you play with us tomorrow." I only found this out because one day after school I asked Kendall what she did at recess, and she said "I just walked around, but I hope tomorrow Sarah lets me play with her and Morgan." Of course my Mama Bear instincts kicked in and I was upset. I had to take a deep breath, wonder to myself who the heck Sarah thinks she is that she can treat my baby this way, and then do a little more digging. I asked what that meant and how many times this has happened. Then I asked, quite nonchalantly, what Kendall thought about this. She said she didn't like it but Sarah only likes to play with one friend at a time so she just had to wait her turn. Now it was a little difficult to think over the screaming going on in my head, but I knew this was a teachable moment for Kendall.

By the time they are tweens, it is difficult to say anything negative about their friends. While it may seem logical and beneficial to tell your tween that a certain friend is not making nice choices and should be avoided, this can actually be fear-provoking in her. I've talked about how important friends are at this age, so the thought of losing a friend – even one who is not especially nice to her – can feel very scary. For the girl who has lots of friends, it can feel as if the delicate balance of her budding circle of friends will be disrupted. And for the girl who tends to just have one or two friends, the thought of being alone can feel intimidating and lonely. When I was young, I tended to have just one friend at a time. I vividly remember the feeling of discovering that my one friend was absent from school and dreading the rest of the day, especially lunch and recess, knowing that I would have to be by myself. Do not underestimate the importance of friends and the impact that suggesting your daughter stop socializing with a certain girl or girls can have on her comfort level.

Back to the issue with Sarah and Kendall. I couldn't just tell her that she needs to drop Sarah as a friend, but I wanted her to know that it wasn't okay to be treated this way. Our conversation went something like this:

Kendall: I just walked around at recess today, but Sarah said I might be able to play with her tomorrow.

Mom: That's too bad, honey, it sounds like recess wasn't very fun today.

K: It wasn't. I wish Morgan never came to my class.

M: I'll bet; this is so hard for you! What did you say to Sarah when she told you that you couldn't play, and that she would decide about tomorrow?

K: I just told her okay.

M: What do you think Sarah learned about you from this?

K: That she gets to be the boss of me.

M: Is that what you want?

K: (rolling eyes) No!

M: Do you wish you had told her something different?

K: Maybe that I don't care and that I'm going to play with Caley instead.

M: I like that! It makes me sad that Sarah thinks she gets to decide what you do at recess. What would happen if tomorrow you just find someone else to play with, maybe Caley? And then if Sarah says that you can play with her, you can tell her that you are playing with Caley, but she can play too if she wants?

K: I think she would be MAD!

M: Maybe. But how could you tell her that you want to play with her and be friends, but she can't pick which days you play, that it hurts your feelings?

K: Maybe you could tell my teacher to tell her? (What can I say, the kid hates confrontation.)

M: Well, I can see how that would be easier. But if you tell her yourself then she'll know that you mean it, and maybe she'll learn that she needs to treat you better.

K: I'll try. Maybe she'll still be happy that I didn't try to not let her play with me and Caley!

I don't want to completely dissect this conversation, but I'd like to point out a few things. First, as with many conversations, I have about ten things going on when Kendall is talking to me. I'm thinking about what's for dinner, paying bills, doing laundry... you can no doubt finish the list because you know exactly what I'm talking about. We're busy! It would have been very easy for me to tell Kendall that recess stunk because Sarah is a jerk and she should just forget about her and find someone else to hang out with. But this keeps me from learning what Kendall really feels when things happen to her, keeps her from learning that she is capable of handling problems, and shows her that I am not really interested in understanding her world from her point of view.

Another notable point of this conversation is that I did not shut down anything that Kendall said. When she said "I wish Morgan never came to my class," I could have said "this isn't Morgan's fault" or "that's not very nice," but this was not the time to point that out. In a pick-your-battles sort of way, I chose to keep focus on Kendall's feelings and the problem at hand, not the out of context point of blame in the situation.

I can't emphasize enough the idea of listening more than you talk. In this situation, I had an idea of what I thought should happen. It bothered me that Kendall could be pushed to the side this way and that she would allow it to happen. It was important to me that she realize she deserved to be treated better and that she feel confident enough to stand up for herself. But I know that just demanding that she realize these things and act accordingly will not work. Listening to her and walking her through the event of the day helped me gauge her feelings and allowed me to help her in a way that makes sense for her. As a case in point, I didn't realize how sensitive she was to the possibility of Sarah getting mad at her. From listening to her, I discovered that she had strong feelings about what was going on, but was afraid to voice them. Through this discovery, I was able to help her find her voice in a way that honored this fear. It was important to tell her friend what she needed, but we could find a way to do it that fits her personality.

In the scenario with Sarah, I felt that I needed to intervene because I saw that Kendall did not realize she had the power to ask to be treated better. But there are plenty of times that the stories your tween comes home with do not require any involvement on your part. In these cases, it is best to simply validate what your daughter is saying. If she says that another girl told her that her lunch looked gross and she was embarrassed, for example, you could probably come up with ideas of what she should have said or could do in the future. But these instances also present an ideal time to show your daughter that you hear her, plain and simple. "It sounds like you felt embarrassed when Rachel made fun of your lunch. I'll bet that made you feel like everyone was watching you eat after that, that doesn't sound fun at all." Your daughter didn't really need to do anything about this situation, and neither did you. She will just feel better getting it off of her chest and knowing that you really *get* why this was a bad thing for her.

In part II we will talk a lot about friendship groups, also known as cliques. But I would like to take a moment to say that as your daughter begins to increase the value she places on friends, remind yourself to enjoy this time. The good times that friends bring don't require any work on your part, so naturally I'm speaking more about the problems that come along with tween friendships, but this is a fun time for your daughter. At its best, these friendships light up her days and become a big part of what she looks forward to each day. I love when Kendall has sleepovers and I hear the non-stop talking, giggling, and silliness. If you strive with your tween to have more of these moments and fewer upsets, you both will do just fine!

Kendall's Corner: In another writing assignment for this book, I wrote this at age 10: A nice, good friend is nice, fun, funny, silly, and doesn't get in trouble much. There are always popular girls. Now some are nice, but others try to get people, and especially the boys, to notice them and make friends. And some are not trying to make friends – they are just naturally mean. A friend is always there for you.

Written at age 11: So in the tween years friends get in lots of fights! But eventually we make up. One of my friends is never mean to me and we hardly fight. But another one of my friends is mean to me a lot. So I have to stick up for myself. She tries to not let me have any friends besides her. And she always calls me and tells me I can't hang up. It's hard to always have to stick up for myself but I don't think she'll leave me alone no matter what.

Chapter 5
Friends – Part II

Have you already seen some cliques forming in your daughter's school or other activities? Because there are so many variables including class size, make up, and personality differences of girls, cliques can start to form at any time during the tween years. They tend to become more defined toward the end of the tween years, but cliques can certainly form early on. I have had many friends complain to me that their fourth grader (or even younger) was coming home with stories that amounted to cliques forming in class (or dance, or soccer...).

The word clique tends to have a negative connotation, reminding us of the circle of mean girls who set out to exclude and torture the girls not in their group. Groups among tweens can run along a large spectrum, ranging from loosely formed groups with members coming in and out, to a tight circle of girls with very defined criteria designed to keep others out. For the sake of simplicity, and to not get sidetracked by the word clique, I am just going to refer to all of the groups along the spectrum as groups. I have always been fascinated by group dynamics, so I tend to drive Kendall crazy with observations and questions about what is going on in the groups around her. You don't need to get overly excited about groups, but it will help you immensely to understand the basic setup that your daughter is in or around.

Think of your adult life, and the groups that are around you. Have you ever noticed that as soon as a group is formed, the same thing tends to happen each time? Imagine your department at work, book club, PTA, Bible study, or any group to which you belong. The group is formed, everyone meets and is nice, and then very soon everyone tends to fall into their roles – someone takes charge and starts to define the rules and give orders, someone echoes the opinions of the person in charge, there are those who are happy to follow along, and usually someone who is not completely invested in the group and is happy to be in the group but could be just as happy out of it.

Tween groups often run the same course of roles and dynamics that I just described. It is simply human nature to fall into the roles that suit our personalities. You probably won't see a group where everyone is in charge, right? Likewise, you aren't likely to see a group where no one is taking charge and everyone is waiting around for someone to take the lead. Have you ever seen the movie *Mean Girls*? It's a funny and exaggerated look at this concept, but it actually represents group dynamics and roles fairly accurately. Let's look at some general categories that girls, and most groups for that matter, fall into. Consider if any of these girls sound like your daughter or girls you know, and then we'll talk about how to use this information in parenting your tween.

Leadership Roles

There is usually a girl who has assumed top-dog position for the group. She decides what and who is cool and basically runs the show. If she's feeling insecure about her position in the group, she may manipulate and diminish the friendships of the girls around her. This allows her to strengthen her position, as the other girls question their friendships with others and become somewhat dependent on the leader for validation.

In many cases, the top-dog has a girl that tries very hard to emulate her. She often follows orders without question; this can be anything from following fashion dictates to icing out other girls that the leader doesn't like. The worst part about this type of girl is that she relies on the leader for friendship and status, so she can be willing to do just about anything to remain in her good graces.

Roles of Obligation/Stuck in the Middle

It's hard for these girls to find their own identity separate from the group. There are many ways that girls in the middle of the pack attempt to remain members of this group. She can serve as the go-between or messenger between her group and another group or person. Another way that girls can try to remain relevant in their group is to spread gossip about others inside or outside of the group, and then use this information as necessary. Of course, this can be hurtful to other girls because their personal information may be used in order for this girl to please the leaders of her group.

I remember watching Kendall's class outside before school one morning when she was in fifth grade. The top-dog in another group whispered something to another girl, who came over and said something snide to Kendall, and then went back and reported what she had done to the giggles of the rest of the group. It was heartbreaking to see, but not out of the ordinary by any means.

Lately there has been a push in the anti-bullying movement to identify the bystanders. These kids are the ones who witness much, but may say little. Likewise, in tween girl groups, the bystander is often caught in the middle of conflict. She is torn about what is going on, and is unsure of the right thing to do. Her conscience may eat at her, but she is likely scared to speak up for fear of being ousted from the group.

Less Invested Group Members

There are girls that are sort of on the fringe of a group, either by choice or as determined by the group. Sadly, there is usually a girl set up by the leaders and others to be the victim. Having a target serves as an example to others of the group's power. This girl can be a member of the group, or the group might select a girl outside of it. This is always so hard to see, because there are always girls who want to be friends with the rest of these girls so badly that they take the abuse or rationalize it.

A girl who has less to lose in the group is something of a drifter. I would say she is usually the best adjusted girl in the group or groups. She is well-liked enough to be welcome in the group, but tends to have friends in different groups and can bop around between groups. Because of this, she usually feels less pressure to be mean or do things she knows are wrong.

While all groups have their unique characteristics, the roles of leaders, middle-of-the-packers, and fringe-girls are usually found to some extent. There is a book called *Queen Bees and Wannabes* by Rosalind Wiseman (18) that identifies several specific roles and goes into detail about how these roles will generally present themselves. If you feel that your daughter is really struggling with the group mentality, it's a great read.

Every time I talk at parenting classes or just informally about the roles within groups, I get a little depressed. These descriptions strike me as so sinister, yet people almost always tell me that they recognize many of their tweens or tween's friends in these categories. And it's important to note that the roles aren't always filled in awful ways. As with most personalities, there is a range of severity here.

Often, we hear stories about what's going on at school and worry about how our daughters are feeling about themselves and treating others, and we wonder how this compares to other girls. Without a strong frame of reference, it can be confusing to know if our daughter's behavior is normal or concerning. Once group systems are broken down in this way, I have seen many parents realize with sadness that their daughter is serving a negative role in her group.

But let's not despair! I believe that awareness leads to understanding and change. I'm hoping that after you read the descriptions, you felt a little relief that there is some sort of order in the chaotic tween scene. Once you understand that there are reasons and explanations for some of the episodes that are happening, you will be better equipped to support your daughter.

As mentioned, all groups are not created equal, each group and each girl is unique. Don't discount a description of a group role because it doesn't fit to a 't.' It is also important to note that these roles aren't permanent, and girls are not locked into these roles for the rest of their lives. The girl who was thought of as top-dog in Kendall's elementary school suddenly found herself the small fish in a big pond in middle school and was quickly demoted; she struggled to find a place to fit in with a new, larger crowd.

Decode Groups for Your Daughter

Because tweens place so much importance on their friends and groups of friends, they can become all-encompassing. For your daughter, this group of girls can feel like her whole world. This helps explain why it's so devastating when friendships fizzle or drama flares up – she's not thinking that this is temporary and in a few years she won't even remember most of this, she's thinking that her world is crumbling around her. It can really help to talk to her about the dynamics of groups and the roles discussed above in order to view the social scene in a different, more logical way. I will warn you, this could be one of those conversations that induces eye-rolling from your tween. There's no need for a formal presentation about the roles within a group, a casual but direct conversation will do just fine.

I don't suggest bringing this up during a tween crisis, instead introduce the topic during dinner, a car ride, or during other quiet moments as something you just heard about and found interesting. Talk about how, even though groups are made up of such different people, there tend to be similar characteristics that play out. Then just as I did, briefly describe each role, making sure to do so in a matter of fact way. In other words, don't say "there are girls who are so desperate to be like the leader of the group that they don't even have a mind of their own." This will only make her defensive when you talk about the roles played by her friends, and puts a negative spin on the whole thing. Be as non-judgmental as possible.

Once you have described the group roles, ask which of her friends fits into those categories. You may need to break things down a bit to get the ball rolling. Instead of asking who she thinks the girls are who look to oblige the leaders, ask which of her friends tends to know the most about the other girls. She may not grasp the title, but she will grasp the meaning.

What is the purpose of asking her about this? I mentioned the benefit of getting her to see her group of friends from a different perspective – hopefully one that will provide a different perception of her social circle that provides her with a broader worldview. But defining which friends fill which roles can really reframe the events of her days. I went over this information with Kendall not long after she started sixth grade. It did take a little rewording to get her to fully engage. She was not willing to identify anyone as a leader because she didn't think anyone was mean. But when I asked who tended to make the most decisions about what the girls would do or wear, she easily identified this person. From there, I was surprised how accurately she recognized the roles within her group.

The tricky part came when discussing the girl who is usually victimized. Kerri is a girl who wants to be friends with the girls in Kendall's group. She does things that 'annoy' Kendall and I hear frequent complaints about her. When we discussed the girl who is usually targeted by her group, Kendall reluctantly named Kerri. There were two important points that I wanted Kendall to understand. First, I pointed out that it's never okay to make anyone feel badly about themselves. This is pure, important, and timeless advice.

But I found out there was a catch to this. I had spent many years telling Kendall not to let anyone be mean to her or bother her. And of course this is good advice – stick up for yourself, say something when someone is bothering you, etc. What I did not clarify is that someone with a personality trait or habit that you find irritating does not represent a bothersome person in the way that I meant. So from Kendall's viewpoint, here is this girl who annoys her. She has two voices echoing in her head, one telling her that you are not supposed to be mean to anyone, and one telling her not to allow anyone to bother her. I must admit that I discovered in a few cases that Kendall chose to not be as nice to this girl as she should have. And worse, she allowed other friends to say mean things without stopping them and joined in when talking about Kerri behind her back.

This leads into the second thing that I wanted Kendall to know. What she was feeling and doing in these situations was totally normal. I said "when you and the other girls were talking about Kerri (without her there), you probably felt kind of good, right? Like you guys had this thing that you shared and it proved to you that you were all friends?" She admitted that yes, that was how it felt. I told her that was totally normal, and it makes sense why she would feel that way. But I also told her that once she realizes how this group setup works, I hope she would understand why it was not okay. And most importantly, I told her that even though it's quite common to bond over the exclusion of someone else, that is never okay.

We talked more about what it must be like to be Kerri. How she tries so hard to be included in this group, and is not treated well. And that this just makes her try harder, which allows everyone else to treat her even worse. Imagining the feelings and thoughts of someone else never stops working, and I do it often. Usually I ask something like this: "Think of how Kerri was treated today, really think about it. Now picture that she gets home from school and her parents ask her how her day was, what do you think she says? She has to either relive the hurts of the day, or she chooses to pretend nothing was wrong because she doesn't want to talk about it, and then goes to sleep dealing with the hurt in her heart all by herself." Asking 'how do you think so-and-so feels' is fine, but putting the situation in a specific context like envisioning what happens when the other person gets home may make the point a little more concrete.

The day after we talked about the roles within groups, I asked Kendall if she noticed anything different. She said the main difference was that when she was observing the activities of another group of girls, she could pick out who was acting in what role. This made them seem less like the 'popular' group and more like real people trying to make sure they stay important.

I also asked what happened with Kerri, and she said "well, you sucked all the fun out of not liking her." A deeper questioning of this comment brought out that Kendall could see that Kerri might be annoying, but had to admit that she wasn't a mean person and didn't deserve to be treated poorly. She also told me, because this was my fault as well, that the secure and even happy feeling that she got from friends who also disliked Kerri lost its luster. Once she heard that it was not okay to bond with friends at the exclusion of someone else, she could not un-ring that bell. I realize that this story does not make Kendall look very nice. I tell you this because this story makes her very much a normal tween. She is actually regarded as a very kind, sweet girl (and no, not just by me and her dad, by teachers and others!). But she is learning, along with every other tween girl, how to plot her course through these years. It is never flawless, and it is never perfect. She struggles to make the right decision sometimes, and I struggle to know what to tell her.

You Know What Role Your Daughter Plays, Now What?

So you've talked the role of groups over with your daughter, and you have decided which role describes her best. What do you do with that information? The simple answer is to find out whether or not this role is serving your daughter well. Start by asking her what her identified role looks like in her daily life. If she said she feels like she is often a bystander to bad behavior, ask her to describe an instance where that played out.

I was speaking to a friend about the concept of groups and she told me later that she went home and tried this advice out. After talking for a while with her daughter Allison, she was sad to discover that Allison felt as if she was the victim in her group. When asked for an example of why she felt this way, she described how she started middle school (sixth grade) assuming she would hang out with the same group of girls she had been friends with in elementary school. It didn't take long before the group shifted a bit, a few girls had gone to different middle schools, and most of the girls had made friends with a few new girls that they met.

Apparently, the new girls (who had become the leaders of the group) had decided that they all could and should be the most popular group at school. Allison was deemed to be not very cool, so these new girls started getting the other girls to be mean to her and excluding her from everything from lunch to text messages to sleepovers. There were a couple of girls (bystanders) who felt badly for Allison, and still liked her. They tried to be nice to her and talk to her, but only when the other girls weren't around. In a way, this made it harder for Allison because she felt like she still had these friends and was essentially being strung along.

My friend was stunned. She had no idea this was even going on. She had noticed that Allison was occasionally moody or upset at home, but chalked it up to hormones because every time she asked if everything was okay, the answer was always yes. And nothing ever came up when Allison was asked how school was that day. Sometimes we feel that if we pepper our tweens with questions, we will find out everything we need to know. The truth is sometimes we need to ask questions in a different way, and sometimes we just need to not ask any questions at all, but give them space to talk. In this case, my friend provided the framework of group dynamics, and provided Allison with enough space to feel comfortable sharing this difficult situation.

As with Allison, sometimes you will discover that your daughter is in a role that is not great for her. Whether she is victimized, being less than nice to other girls, or standing by while others are mean, it can be difficult to accept that your daughter is anything less than the sweet angel you had envisioned. I can recall only one person telling me that she believed her daughter to be a leader who was less than kind. Almost everyone else either rationalizes what they know or learn about their daughter ("she's just a natural leader, and sometimes people take that the wrong way"), or they remain unsure about where she fits in. When I found out how Kendall was treating Kerri, even I found myself initially scrambling to explain it away. If you are feeling disappointed in the choices your tween is making, realize that it doesn't mean she is a bad kid, it means she is perhaps making bad choices. And also understand that she is perfectly normal, and that burying your head in the sand is not going to allow you to support her going forward.

Talking with your tween about her place in her group of friends is a great jumping off point. You are coming at the issue from the framework of the group information, not just pulling her behavior out of thin air. It would be ideal if she clearly identifies as the role that accurately describes her. Of course your tween may not acknowledge her actual role in the group. If, despite you describing each role in a very non-judgmental and positive way, she still sees her role as negative, she may not fess up to serving in this position. Let's say you know that she tries desperately to please the leader of her group, but she is reluctant to admit this. There's no need to convince her that she has an official role in her group, or brow beat her until she admits it. Not productive and not necessary. Whether she clearly identifies as a specific role or is reluctant to be labeled, you can ask some open-ended questions that will help her identify what she likes about herself, what she may wish to change, and what she may not have been aware of. Great questions to start with are questions such as:

If someone asked your friends to describe you, what do you hope they would say (even if you don't think it's realistic, what do you wish they would say)?

What do you think they would actually say?

What is your favorite thing about your group of friends?

If you could change one thing about your group of friends, what would it be?

Think of a girl who most of your friends don't like. Who would be the most likely to get someone else to say something mean to her? Who would be the most likely to feel badly for her? Who would be the most likely to pretend to be her friend but then talk about her behind her back?

Imagine that everyone is being mean to a certain girl, what do you think the right thing is to do in that situation? How hard would it be to stand up for that girl and tell your friends to leave her alone – especially if you don't really like her either? How would you feel after you did that?

What is one thing that you did today that made you feel proud of yourself?

What is one thing that you did today that made you wish you had done something different?

What is your best quality? Do you feel like you get to use that quality a lot?

Is there anything that you could do that would make you deserve to be treated badly by others?

Talking to your tween is an ongoing conversation. Don't throw all of these questions at her in one sitting. As moments present themselves, dole them out over time. If you have these types of questions in mind, you will undoubtedly find moments to ask them. Your tween will be talking to you about things that happened during her day, and you'll find a way to ask her something. Or if she has or is becoming a bit tight-lipped about her days, she will at least mention the name of a friend or classmate, again opening the door to ask her things.

Don't Miss an Opportunity to Say Nothing

Remember, just as we talked about in chapter 4, there are many times to just keep quiet. This is very difficult for me, and probably a lot of you. More than once, Kendall has told me "you know mom, everything doesn't have to be a lesson." The problem is that if she is sharing a problem or situation with me, I see opportunities to share solutions with her, point out what she might have done differently, or explain why someone is not acting appropriately, etc. It is very difficult to not give my two cents on the situation (apparently, I have this same problem with my husband, but I don't see this changing anytime soon – sorry honey).

Even if you have a great suggestion, it is okay to keep it to yourself. Kendall comes home almost daily with a story of what someone did to her, or what someone did to someone else. Obviously, if someone was a danger to themselves or others, it would require a report. But most of the time, these stories require no action on my part other than taking an interest in her day, and being a good listener. If a boy said something annoying, friends are arguing, or someone misbehaved during class, sometimes all I need to do is commiserate with her or ask what happened next.

This boils down to the skill of discernment. As I listen to Kendall, I tend to ask myself a couple of questions. Am I starting to see a pattern form? In other words, does it seem that most days contain a story about the same girl picking on others? Does it seem that Kendall is taking on negative behaviors – perhaps signaling an unfavorable role within her group of friends? The bottom line is that random happenings do not generally require commentary and specific direction from you. Emerging trends and problematic behaviors are your cue that your daughter needs some guidance from you. Let's take a look at how to focus this guidance.

Begin by Knowing What You Want to Accomplish, but Be Open to Learning New Things

It is very helpful to know your end game with your daughter. If you know she is becoming something of a follower and not making positive, independent choices, be aware of what you want for her. Remember Kendall's issue with Sarah? I knew that I wanted her to be better about standing up for herself, so my questions highlighted that area. But in talking with her, I realized just how much she hated conflict and how unsettled she became at the thought of someone being mad at her. So I came at the situation with the goal of empowering her to stand up to Sarah, but was open enough to hear her concerns about making Sarah mad.

If your daughter is often trying to oblige others in her group, you may want to direct your line of questioning around why she is willing to do what others want her to do without question, and what problems this might be causing her. But make sure to listen to her as well, you may be surprised to learn that she never wanted to be in this role but felt too vulnerable to change it and is now pigeon-holed into this role. Or you may find out that she is in a get-them-before-they-get-me state of mind; she is willing to act a certain way in order to (she thinks) guard herself from being ousted from the group or treated poorly.

Bring it Back to the Foundation

You must have known that you hadn't heard the last of the mission statement, vision board, or whatever you came up with! This is just a friendly reminder that if your daughter is struggling with her role within her group, these are tools that can help her clarify whether or not this 'title' is something that she wants for herself. If her mission statement says that she wants to be thought of as a kind and helpful person, but she is acting in a mean way as a leader, ask her what she has done – or not done – to contribute to being kind and helpful. This is not a cross-examination of her choices, holding up her mission statement and demanding to know how it syncs up with her recent behavior. It is another angle from which you can explore what is going on in her world, meant to serve as a gentle reminder of the direction she would like her life to go. After all, these are her words, not yours. This can help her take more ownership of what is going on.

When Looking to Make Changes, Think Small

I am a huge fan of the 'one small thing' approach to many issues. When I strive to eat healthier, I don't go overboard. When I thought we might be eating too much sugar in our house, I didn't go sugar-free, I started out by not adding sugar to my tea, and choosing desserts that have more fruit or nuts and less sugar and chocolate, and then slowly looking for other opportunities to swap foods out. I have the same philosophy with behavior change. Because Kendall hates conflict and is not willing to confront people, I would not tell her that she needs to jump in the middle of an argument and confront the aggressor with demands to stop what they are doing. Instead, we would talk about why it's not okay to stand by and let someone be mistreated. Then I would ask her what she could do to stop this. Sometimes, your daughter might have some great ideas in mind, and sometimes she will need some inspiration. Whether your daughter is frequently picked on, or the one doing the picking, break the problem down and find small ways that she can begin to modify any harmful behaviors.

In Kendall's case, she has come up with more diversion tactics than confrontations. Her idea is to find a way to change the subject or divert attention – if girls are being mean to another girl Kendall may pretend she sees a teacher coming around a corner, and then say "oh, I'm glad that wasn't Mrs.

Smith, I didn't want you to get in trouble because you shouldn't be doing this." And then before things heat up again, finding a reason to break up the group, either by telling her friend that she had something to show her somewhere else, or by telling the person being picked on (assuming it's not her friend) that she thinks she may have dropped something over by the lunchroom door. Now this is not the neat and tidy picture I would like to envision Kendall conducting, but that's the thing, Kendall's personality does not lend itself to a grand, heroic moment. And these are kids, so to expect them to be logical, benevolent, and articulate during times of conflict is not realistic. By listening to her, I discovered that she was able to come up with some unorthodox yet effective means of solving problems.

A great way to make sure she is prepared to try new behaviors out is to role play them. I can almost guarantee that there may be some eye rolling at this suggestion, but I promise it will be worth it. We have role played specific issues, such as a questionable 'friend' who started to ridicule Kendall in order to look cool to others. We talked about her options when this happened. Either her dad or I would pretend to be this other girl, and she would try out the different options. It really did help to get her comfortable having these words and serious tone come out of her mouth.

We have also done role playing in order to address issues that may not have happened but were likely to come up, such as someone trying to get her to do something mean to someone else, or a boy trying to engage her in an inappropriate conversation. In addition to the actual events in Kendall's life, I would hear someone else talking about an incident with their tween or see something on television, and I would jot it down on a small square of paper. Like drawing names out of a hat, we keep the squares of paper in a basket on the dining room table. During dinners or free time, we role play them with her. Not so much that it is annoying, but enough to cover some basic topics.

So based on her role in her group of friends, you may discover a theme of behaviors to cover – if she is something of a gossip, you may find that she needs to learn and practice the art of discretion and become aware of how harmful gossip can be. If she is often victimized, she needs to learn that she needn't endure mistreatment in order to have friends, but the smaller step to that is to teach her small ways to begin to assert her rights to fair and kind treatment.

I would like to clarify that in the next chapter, I will talk about bullying. I realize that some of the stories and concepts we are talking about here have the impression of bullying. When I have spoken on the topic of parenting tweens, the most exasperated parents that come up to me for specific help are the ones who are dealing with bullying situations, and I feel that it warrants its own chapter. So if you are reading this chapter and wishing for more coverage of help related to bullies, or wondering how to decipher between typical conflicts and bullying, help is just a few pages away. Some of the advice given here will be echoed in terms of dealing with a bully. But certainly there are some specific characteristics of bullying that require specific definitions and intervention.

Think Small (Yes, Again)

If things are going great for your tween, there's no need to try and change things. It is still helpful to decode the group roles so that she has a new awareness of how things work in her world. This insight also makes her attentive to problems should they arise, and may also help alert her to any negativity in other groups of girls. This becomes especially helpful if she has the opportunity to stand up for the target of another group, or simply other girls who are being mistreated.

More than likely, however, your daughter is or will be experiencing some negative effects of tween group dynamics. In this case, your goal is not to dismantle the entire group system and foundation of your daughter's social environment (see think small, above!). If you are not a fan of her social circle, it is tempting to just want her out of the group she's in so that she can seek out nicer girls. Remembering how scary it can be for girls to lose their friends or their social status, you already know that this is not the way to go about changing things.

If you feel as if things aren't going very well for your daughter, or you worry about the group she is friends with, little changes can make a big difference. But you need to be realistic about the changes you would like to see. To start, find the positives of the role that she is in. Kids don't land in these roles entirely by accident. There is *something* about this role that rings true to her personality. If she's a leader, does she have natural leadership qualities? As a bystander, does she have a difficult time making quick decisions because of her sweet nature? Look at the skills involved in the role that she plays, and find the positive aspects of them. You know her best, so you will know how to find the encouraging features in your daughter's behavior.

Once you have decided what you are working with you can work at things from both offensive and defensive standpoints. First, make sure to bolster her confidence and build on skills that will allow her to stand up for herself when necessary. This, again, is where you know your daughter best. A quiet, sweet natured girl is not likely to stand up eye-to-eye with a bully and shout "leave me alone!" Instead, you need to find something that she *is* likely to do. Kendall is not quiet by any stretch, but as you've been learning, she is not confrontational. With her, we came up with lots of ideas – mainly from our role plays, that she felt comfortable doing or saying. Brainstorm all kinds of things to say and do, and practice the ones that feel right to her.

As I mentioned, if I see a television show presenting a conflict between friends, I will make note of it and write it down as a discussion or role play topic to be put in the basket. For example, I remember a program in which one character confides in her friend that her family is having financial trouble. Later, when the character begins to brag about how much the clothes that she is wearing cost, the friend tells all of their other friends about this family's problems. We talked about which role the gossip was acting in, why the gossip was likely tempted to spill this information, what Kendall would have done if she knew someone was having money problems but boasted about material possessions, and role played what she could do if she was a bystander to this situation. Kendall felt that, being able to imagine the girl's embarrassment and hurt at being betrayed, she would be able to say to the gossip that what she had done was not nice and not okay. And then, she intended to quickly change the subject to something else that was going on in the world.

Second, make sure you are not just looking at what is being done to your daughter, look at what she is doing to others. If your daughter tends to be a gossip, talk with her about how hurtful that can be. Acknowledge the feeling of power and/or bonding with other girls that it likely gives her, but explain why it is not okay. Again, brainstorm ideas with her of what she could do instead. When she feels the urge to spill the beans about something she knows about someone else, how about a goal of either saying something nice about that person instead, or saying nothing at all. If she comes home having done this, or something similar, praise her for her great choice. Talk through what happened, noting what was great about it and what was challenging. If she has done something different than normal in the group, perhaps the leaders are confused or even upset by the lack of information coming from your daughter. Recognize this shift in their relationship.

No matter what the concern that you are addressing with your tween, it is important to tackle it in these small pieces. Look at what she does and what others do to her to make sure that she is able to stand up for herself, but is also not causing hurt feelings in others. Small changes do begin to add up and have a ripple effect. Your daughter will learn how and when to stand up for herself, what she is doing that might be hurting others and why she was doing it, and what she can do instead that is positive and more in line with the girl that she wants to be (and perhaps already is deep down). Not long after giving up sugar in my tea, I began finding that I didn't need to dust French toast with powdered sugar and many other opportunities to avoid sugar. Before long we were trying fruit instead of dessert! Ok, that last one didn't work out, but the point remains – one small change can result in more and more meaningful changes.

Don't Label Her

One of my pet peeves is when people announce a perceived characteristic of their child to others, especially in the presence of their child. Two friends with preschoolers will run into each other at the grocery store with their children in tow, and when one is asked about her day, she answers "well you know he drives me crazy, he is going to be wild in here and end up in trouble!" Or to combat a picky eater, what do parents do? Announce at every meal that their child is a picky eater! As they get older, parents tend to do the same thing with their tweens. How many times have you heard someone say "we butt heads all the time" or "she's such a drama queen about everything" in the presence of their tween? I will concede that in the grand scheme of things, these are not events that will scar and traumatize our tweens for life. But these comments set a tone, level of expectation, and tell our tweens what we really think of them. And children often live up to the expectations that we set for them.

From toddlers to tweens, sometimes we make these statements as a pre-emptive strike, right? If mom doesn't think she will be able to stop little Sally from freaking out when she is denied a candy bar at the store, she will tell people "oh my Sally is a little spit-fire!" on their way in. This way, when Sally does in fact freak out, mom can at least be comforted by the fact that she was right. Or perhaps you want to make sure no one can beat you to the punch. If mom has announced that little Judy runs wild at birthday parties, and she does, mom doesn't have to worry that another mom will say "wow, Judy is so hyper" because she can say "I already told you that!"

All kids internalize what we say about them, and this will still be the case as your tween gets older. And if you have said the same thing for years, well, you need to really look at what message that has sent. Many times moms will speak about their children in labels to other parents: "Well Mackenzie is my shy one and Lauren is my wild child." Or have you ever been in your daughter's classroom and realized how quickly you could figure out who the 'troublemakers' were? Of course the behavior of some children makes it easy to identify them as ones who are often in trouble, but it always bothered me that these children were so often labeled as such. Hearing a teacher say to a student "you will keep being sent to the corner until you stop being such a pest" seems like a logical consequence. And I am certainly not vilifying teachers, but said several times in several ways, this child – and his peers – learn that she IS a pest. She isn't hearing "I loved it when you were working quietly on your worksheet, your handwriting is awesome, I wonder what happened? You need to sit in the corner for a few minutes so that you can remember how to be the great student that I know you are." See the difference? It's the same with you: are you giving your daughter a label to live up to – or down to?

You may be just starting the evolution of the value that your daughter places on friends, or you may be in the thick of the magnitude of tween friendships. No matter where you are in this process, your daughter is still wanting and needing your guidance. The number and variety of issues that come up for tween friendships can feel overwhelming. If you can remember that your role really boils down to a few themes, you will manage just fine. Remember that your tween has enough girls to say "omg – I can't even believe she did that," meaning she doesn't need another tween, she needs a mom. As a mom, you can be a great listener. Validate what she is feeling, celebrate when things are fantastic, and commiserate when things aren't going well. Don't apply labels to her that only serve to paint her into a corner. Offer suggestions and role play scenarios when you start to notice negative behaviors or patterns, either of other girls consistently treating her poorly or of her engaging in bad behavior of her own.

Make sure you understand the basic structure of groups and the roles girls play within them. Find ways to help her understand what is going on in her friendship groups so that she can identify the why's and how's of what her and her friends are doing. And remember that, typically, none of this requires massive and sweeping changes, small changes in what your daughter says and does can have a big impact.

Kendall's Corner: I hate drama... but it's still good to have girl friends that you know will never betray you and will accept you for you. I hope your girls listen up and talk to you! Sometimes it is boring to listen to the stories but in the end you will realize it happens to everyone and parents will probably have good advice!! Sometimes I realize how much less drama there is when I spend time with guys (who are just my friends).

My mom wrote about the role plays. I admit that they help, I feel like I've played out a scene already when it happens.

But I noticed that she said we don't do them so much that it's annoying and, well...

I watched an old episode of the television show *The King of Queens*. In it, Carrie had taken a seasonal job where Doug works. She told Doug that she was so excited after having a few days to get to know her co-workers that she had already made a best friend – and found a girl they both hated. This reminded me of what my mom said about how it's normal to bond with other people by leaving someone else out. This just proves you are going to struggle with drama and mean girls your whole life!!

Chapter 6
Bullying

This is a topic that can become alarming for so many of us. While working on this book, I heard numerous news stories about the devastating effects of bullying. Each time, I would get upset and run to the computer so that I could write something that would hopefully help someone. It's a helpless and frustrating feeling, wanting to say just the right thing to trigger just the right changes that will help resolve the problem of bullying. Of course it's not that simple, and it made me realize that most of us share the frustration around this problem. When we hear of a child who commits suicide after enduring months or years of bullying, we are collectively outraged, and the feeling of wanting to do something to change the way things are overcomes us all.

I love the saying "be the change you wish to see in the world." (Full disclosure here, this is a quote attributed to Gandhi, though some claim he never said it. Regardless, I actually heard it from an *Oprah* show!) I feel that when difficult subject matter comes up, we have the choice to avoid it and bury our heads, or dive head first into it and do our best to 'be the change.' This is why, as a therapist, I specialized in parenting. It was so difficult to work with children who made great progress in therapy, but then regressed when they went home to parents who lacked parenting skills or had untreated mental illnesses of their own. I dove head first into working with parents in order to support healthier kids, families, and communities. I invite you to do the same regarding the topic of bullying. This chapter will cover a broad range of bully-related topics, but my hope is that reading this chapter will be just a part of your involvement in this area, and that you will join me in 'being the change.' I hope you read more on the subject, speak with other parents, speak with your kids, and find any way you can to get and keep people talking about bullying and what we need to do to protect children.

Defining Bullying

Lately, it seems that the word bully has become the go-to word for any and all conflicts among kids. I can't tell you many times the parents of girls in Kendall's class will report to me that a conflict arose between friends or classmates, and will say that one is bullying the other. The problem with overusing this word is that we begin to become desensitized to it, and it loses the serious classification that it deserves. My aim here is not to start a campaign to encourage proper usage of the term bully, but to point out that bullying describes a distinct set of characteristics. And in order to be recognized and taken seriously by school districts and others should it become necessary, it is a word that needs to carry sufficient weight. For this reason, and for the purposes of having an accurate working definition throughout this chapter, I want to define what bullying is.

According to the website www.stopbullying.gov, bullying is "unwanted, aggressive behavior among school aged children that involves a real or perceived power imbalance. The behavior is repeated, or has the potential to be repeated, over time. Both kids who are bullied and who bully others may have serious, lasting problems." Bullying can include actions such as making threats, spreading rumors, attacking someone physically or verbally, and purposely excluding someone from a group. In order to be considered bullying, the behavior must be aggressive and include:

> -An Imbalance of power. Kids who bully use their power – such as physical strength, access to embarrassing information, or popularity – to control or harm others. Power imbalances can change over time and in different situations, even if they involve the same people.

> -Repetition. Bullying behaviors happen more than once or have the potential to happen more than once. (19)

If I could read your mind for a moment, I would bet that you just imagined a situation that your daughter has been in recently and inserted it into this definition to either confirm or dismiss the possibility that it was a bullying situation. At the very least, the face or faces of some children your daughter knows popped into your head as you read the definition. Now imagine that you are a teacher or school administrator listening to the description of a problem that one child is having with another, and think how difficult it must be to determine whether the term bullying applies. I like this definition, I think it is thorough and accurate. And even though it covers the important elements of bullying, there is no getting around the fact that it is subjective.

In some instances that your daughter either experienced or witnessed, you may have wondered whether this was in fact a bullying incident or if it was just conflict or teasing. And if confronted, the offending girl (or boy), or perhaps a teacher or parent, even defended the actions by claiming that they were simply teasing. Is my daughter being oversensitive? Am I? Am I under-reacting or over-reacting? It is so difficult to know. There are so many differences in the personalities of children and so many varying factors making each situation unique, that determining if the circumstances qualify as bullying can become cloudy.

We've seen a good definition of bullying. So by comparison, here's how I view the categories of teasing and conflict. Teasing is meant to be fun or lighthearted and does not intentionally hurt or humiliate the girl being teased. But most importantly, teasing is a mutual activity, meaning that the teaser and the one being teased often trade roles (or at least the potential exists). Another important note about teasing is that if it gets out of hand and the girl being teased gets upset, the teaser is likely to feel badly and apologize – and stop the teasing.

Conflict is a little more complicated. This is when children disagree or clash with each other about an idea or activity. There is some sort of disagreement or struggle that creates friction and problems between them. The result is an argument or other acting out, perhaps bickering, ignoring, or complaining to others outside of the conflict.

Reading the description of conflict, you may be thinking that conflict seems to have a lot in common with bullying. And you would be right. This is exactly why I think it's so important to really be able to conceptualize what is and is not bullying, and to look at each situation individually. We all want to protect our daughters and prevent harmful relationships from damaging them, so we certainly don't want to become known as the parent who cries bully, keeping us from helping our daughters when they need it most.

As noted, bullying can share components of conflict, including ignoring, excluding, and/or talking about another person to others. And there can certainly be a lot of overlap in teasing, conflict, and bullying. The key difference between them, however, is the power differential and the repetitive nature of the behavior. In a bullying situation, it is important to note the power imbalance between the people involved. Beyond just physical size and strength, power imbalance can be a real or perceived difference in popularity, or even the power one girl may hold over another with information she knows that may embarrass or threaten the other girl.

Think back to how movies used to portray bullies, they were always big, lumbering, and inept. In a rare instance of media getting something right, bullies are now shown in a more accurate light. They look like all of the other girls, can be quite charming and pleasant when necessary, and socially skilled at turning cruel when targeting their victim. Don't assume you will know what a bully looks like, you will never identify one based on appearance.

If I am doing my job right, you are considering the idea that discord among tween girls can take many forms. Perhaps you already knew this but have been swept up in the bullying wave that tends to escalate every situation to a bullying incident. It is also possible that your daughter has been experiencing bullying but other parents or school personnel have tried to downplay it claiming that it is just kids being kids. Or maybe your daughter is just starting to experience difficulties with friends or peers, and you are realizing that every incident is unique. Regardless, I hope that this information allows you to calm yourself and feel confident that you can look at situations that occur with your daughter without panicking.

I must admit that anyone who knows me would read the last sentence about panicking and laugh. Because I *am* the parent who panics when conflicts arise with Kendall. There is often a belief that psychologists are able to view problems with their own children in a Zen and analytical way, and that they are able to mitigate problems with ease. I am a glaring example of this being a false belief. More than once, I have been exasperated and breathlessly told my husband about a situation that is going on with Kendall, and he'll calmly come back with "tell me again what it is that you do for a living?" Funny guy, I know, but he does this to bring me back to reality. I, like some of you, have the personality trait that involves freaking out at the mere hint of unhappiness in our daughters. Despite an awareness that I cannot protect Kendall from the world, and that she actually *needs* to learn the skills of problem solving and conflict resolution, I don't want her to experience hurt feelings and (gasp) tears of sadness.

I tell you this because even if you are not quite as extreme on the panic spectrum as I am, a lot of you do tend to go from zero to sixty when something happens to your daughter. This is totally normal; we go into protective mode and want to take action. Combine this with the current hyper-focus on bullying, and I think what happens is that our daughter comes home reporting a problem with another child, and we instantly think BULLY!

So the next time an issue arises, before you assign any labels to the behavior, do a quick definition check to see if the incident qualifies as teasing or conflict. Or if you know that the behavior rises way above the level of teasing but the offending child, parent, or other adult claims that 'they were just teasing', refer to this definition before letting someone else rationalize behavior that clearly is more significant than teasing or conflict.

How to Bully-Proof Your Tween

There is, of course, no way to guarantee that your daughter will not have to deal with a bully. But there are things that you can do to put the odds in her favor. Here are some effective tools for helping your daughter:

- Talk about bullying. Don't try to hide the issue from her, shine a bright light on it instead. There is no need to saddle her with the differences between teasing, conflict, and bullying; she shouldn't be expected to decipher what is happening to her or around her, this is not realistic. But she should know that she has the right to feel safe in her environment, and to know what it looks like when she is not. Make sure she knows that bullies aren't just people who are bigger or stronger than her, that anyone has the potential to be a bully. Point out examples of bullying that you are aware of, or look for some in television or movies. The more easily your daughter can identify bullying, the more likely she is to talk about it and report it.

- Keep her busy. Ensure that your daughter is involved in activities that she enjoys. Sports, Girl Scouts, youth groups, clubs, or any other activities that she is engaged in will help boost her confidence and improve her social skills. Additionally, it broadens her world. It's easy for tweens to feel that school is their entire world. Help her to realize that if things aren't going well in one area, they may likely be going better in another. The perspective gained from this is very empowering.

- Validate her feelings. Yes, you've heard this before! I can't stress enough that if your daughter knows that when she comes to you with any kind of upset, she will be heard and not judged, you have already done a fantastic job. It does my heart good to think of tweens who have a problem at school and know that when they get home, they will receive a warm welcome and listening ear. And it breaks my heart to think of those who suspect that if they relay this problem, they will be met with the accusation that they are overreacting or are not tough enough, or that they are simply not heard.

- See what she already knows. As I mentioned, it is tempting to rush into finding solutions to your daughter's personal problems. But take a second to find out what she did to attempt to solve the problem when it happened. This will help you gauge what skills you need to work on with her – did she completely freeze and do nothing? Did she make attempts at problem-solving? Did she tell anyone what happened? Finding out what her response

84

to the situation was will point you in the right direction. This also piggybacks onto validating her feelings. If she tells you what happened and you launch into what she should have done or needs to do next time, this robs her of the opportunity to fully vent about her feelings, and also limits her ability to show you what she may have already done or thought about.

- Role play. Later in this chapter, I will talk about some different ways to deal with a bully. Use these to role play situations with your daughter so she is comfortable and familiar with the different strategies available to her.

- Point out the positive. We spend so much time telling our tweens what they *can't* do, it's equally important to tell them what they *can* do. Point out situations that you see or hear about that demonstrate healthy conflict resolution or stopping a bullying situation. Talk about the options that the person in the situation had; perhaps it would have been easier for this person to do something really mean/look the other way/not speak up. Also, role model healthy behavior to your daughter. Kendall (and by extension, me) is involved in many different activity circles – school, friends, softball, basketball, and our neighborhood to name a few. I have asked her if she thought any of the adults in these groups might be bullies, or display bullying behavior. She didn't hesitate to name, quite accurately, which adults acted poorly toward others.

- Make communication a revolving door. Similar to the conversations we've talked about having regarding puberty, we want to make sure that we don't just have one talk about bullying. Having ongoing communication about what goes on in your daughter's world, as well as the world around her, assures her that you are always available. It also allows for the topic to be explored in many different ways in order to be as comprehensive as possible, and come at the problem from different angles. If you hear the story of a bullying situation, tell her about it and ask her what she thinks about it, what she would have done, or if anything similar has happened to her or someone she knows. If you learn about a new tool for her to use in the battle against bullying, talk to her about it and role play it.

Dealing with Reality

Despite our best efforts, your tween is likely to either witness bullying, or perhaps even be faced with a bully herself. Hopefully you now feel more comfortable assessing situations as they arise and can take a deep breath before diving into action. Let's move forward with what to do after you take that breath.

Witnessing Bullying

If your daughter witnesses bullying, it is so important for her to know that she has a role in stopping it. This in no way implies that she is responsible for the bullying or responsible for the outcome. But it is a significant change in our collective mindset to raise children with awareness that when bullying occurs, they have a job to do. The way in which your tween will react will depend largely on the situation, but also on her personality. In chapter 5, we talked about different ways your tween might intervene on a conflict. These tactics apply to bullying as well. When your tween witnesses bullying, she and the others present are known as bystanders. In the struggle to reduce bullying, I cannot emphasize enough the role of empowering the bystander. Bullies thrive when operating unopposed, so putting the spotlight on them and finding more people to say "this is not cool" than people who cheer them on is paramount.

In order to empower bystanders, we need to first make sure they are comfortable helping others. Find ways to encourage your daughter to develop the habit of being a helper. Helping classmates with class work and homework, helping another child who has dropped something to pick it up, offering to take schoolwork to a classmate who is absent, etc. You get the idea; create an environment of helpfulness so that helping becomes second nature and she sees that offering help is a part of her life.

And don't forget to role model this for her. My husband is a great example of someone who helps others. He is the guy who reaches things in the grocery store for elderly people or someone in a wheelchair, he is the guy you see jumping out of his car to help push the car that ran out of gas, and he has been the guy who literally pulled people from a burning car. Now I don't want Kendall putting herself in harm's way to help, and she realizes that her dad is a former football player and able to help in ways that she cannot or should not. But the point is that she has not grown up thinking that 'someone else will help this person.'

I do help people in the grocery store, and quickly jump in when I see a lost child, but I do not have the same run-toward-crazy situations mentality that my husband has. When I saw what looked like a domestic violence situation in a parking lot I did *not* jump out of my car. What I did do is follow the other car while shaking so badly I could barely dial 911. I wanted to show Kendall that while it was not safe for me to intervene, I did find my own way to help. Perhaps you do all of this, and that is wonderful – keep it up with a renewed purpose.

Additionally, continue to teach empathy. We also talked about this in chapter 5, really looking at situations from the other's point of view. And again, I suggest discussing situations in different ways and doing more than just asking "how would you feel if this happened to you." Kendall told me the story of Andrew, a boy in her grade. The class was in the lunchroom and Andrew was goofing around with some of the other boys. The other boys started to tease him, and once his frustration peaked, he attempted to deflect some of the teasing by throwing his water bottle up in the air. One of the other boys caught the water bottle and threw it hard at Andrew, hitting him in the eye. Already frustrated, and now hurt, Andrew started to cry. Luckily, a teacher was in the area and quickly sent all of the kids out to recess (yay, teacher!!), leaving Andrew to collect himself without all of the kids staring at him.

Kendall obviously felt badly for Andrew, enough to tell me the story after school. When I asked her about it, I avoided simply asking how she thought Andrew felt. I asked what she thought he was thinking when he knew everyone was looking at him but he couldn't stop crying. I asked what she would guess his one wish would be in that moment – to not cry and look tough instead? That no one would be around to see him cry? That he never threw the water bottle in the first place? And I asked how long he would probably think about what happened: Everyone saw what happened, but most likely forgot about it by the end of the school day, or only thought about it for a second before going on with their lives.

But what about Andrew? This was awful for him, and he probably thought about it non-stop for the rest of the day, and for a few days after, and then in random moments going forward. And what do you think he told his parents? What do you think they said to him? I wanted her to really get inside Andrew's head and try to relate to his experience. The more your tween can think about another person's situation from a broader perspective, the more deeply she will develop empathy.

Okay, so that's the backdrop to empowerment; you create an atmosphere of helpfulness and empathy so that when the need arises, the impulse to help and do something will kick in. What, then, does empowerment and action look like when your tween witnesses bullying? It will look different for every tween, because every tween is different. We talked in chapter 5 about teaching our tweens to stick up for other kids, and how this approach varies based on personality. This holds true when witnessing bullying. You know your tween best – would she be comfortable being outspoken and asserting herself loudly? If she is quiet, it is not reasonable to expect that she would do this. Teaching your daughter a basic three-step process is the easiest way to set into motion your expectations about stepping in and get her used to what will be involved.

First, she needs to know that she must do something. And I mean drill this into her head, there is not an optional response, but a required one. Think how different the culture of bullying would be if every time it happened, at least one bystander did something. If your tween understands that no matter who else is around she is expected to do something about the situation, then it is not a matter of *if* she can help, but *how* she can help.

Second, she needs to know her options. Again, you know her best. Devise a set of options based on her strengths. As I mentioned before, Kendall is not big on confrontation. I would not try to convince her to loudly confront a bully, she's just not built for that. But she is pretty quick on her feet, and able to think of off-beat comments to distract people or redirect focus. If she was to walk up on a peer being bullied, she is likely to do something like yell "oh my gosh, I just lost my contact! Everybody take two steps back!" or "did the fish sticks at lunch seem weird to anyone else? I totally think I'm going to barf!"

With your tween, brainstorm ideas to create enough of a distraction to stop what is going on. Start her off with an example (like the contact lens) and come up with a bunch. The more practice she has coming up with off the wall ideas, the more comfortable she will be doing it in the spur of the moment. And write them down somewhere, so that from time to time you can look over the list and even role play a few of them. My favorite ones tend to be the one that remove the child being bullied, such as telling them that you found something that belongs to them and need them to come with you in order to claim it, or saying that some teacher asked you to please find that person and bring them to the classroom. These are non-confrontational, but disrupt what is going on.

If your daughter is comfortable being assertive, then practice this approach. Ask her to demonstrate what she would do if she witnessed a bullying situation. Any version of "what you are doing is not okay, knock it off right now" is fantastic. Standing next to the victim is helpful, as is direct eye contact with the bully.

When I talk to Kendall about sticking up for herself or others, I always tell her that she should avoid an exchange of insults. If and when the story is retold, it would be great if the other person's version does not include "well she called me x, y, or z." There is no need to sink to a level that includes name calling or personal attacks; I feel that it only invites the desire for retribution later on. Her goal is to stop the bullying, simple as that. (I will say that I've made sure that Kendall knows that should something unflattering slip out while she is helping another child, she will not be in trouble with us. I would hate to have her not help because she is afraid that she will end up in trouble for a slip of the tongue). And again, removing the victim from the situation is ideal. Stepping in, saying that what is happening is unacceptable, and asking the victim to walk away with her as quickly as possible is the ideal order of events. And again, role play these with your tween at casual times to keep her in practice!

Hopefully these options will work for your tween. But she also needs to know that there are times when she is in over her head. Empowering the bystander does not mean putting her in harm's way. Always assure her that if violence is occurring, if she knows that the bully has a history of violent behavior, or if she just has a bad feeling and doesn't feel that it is safe for her to step in, she does not need to put herself in that situation. I would also add that she may want to avoid stepping in if she is in a remote location, perhaps the end of the school parking lot, or away from quick access to an adult. You won't be surprised to hear that my suggestion is to come up with scenarios that fit this description to help her decipher the appropriate course of action and role play them! In the cases that may prove to be over her head, she should know to immediately find the nearest adult or even call 911 if she is unable to locate an adult.

Third, the incident needs to be reported. Obviously, if your daughter opted to find an adult to intervene in a situation, this is sufficient. But regardless of the option your tween chooses, she needs to be encouraged to report the situation to a teacher or administrator. Younger tweens are often more willing to tell teachers about social problems than older tweens, who begin to worry about the 'snitch' label. If your tween tells you that she does not want to 'tattle' on other kids, this is totally normal. It is important to let her know that you understand the importance of not being the tattle-tale. It is equally important to let her know why it is important to let someone know about bullying, and to know that there are ways to let teachers know without everyone knowing it was her that told. If she can't find a time to talk to the teacher when no one is around, then she needs to let you know so that you can call or e-mail the teacher. And the quicker the better, it is important for these matters to be dealt with swiftly.

If school staff witnessed the situation, perfect, this is on them. If not, then ideally the victim will be the one to report the incident. If your tween witnessed the bullying, she can ask the victim if he/she would like your tween to go with him/her to report it. If the victim says that they do not intend to report it, this is when it is up to your tween to do so.

There is a caveat to the reporting. The tween years are a transition in which the parent-child dynamics are being restructured and refined, and trust is such an important part of this. It can be challenging if your daughter comes home with a report of something happening at school, but then begs you not to make her say anything, or to not say anything yourself. This is a really tough position. If you simply insist that it must be reported, you may lose her trust and prevent her from telling you things in the future. As important as I believe reporting things is, trust between you and your daughter is paramount.

If she asks you to not say anything, do not freak her out by saying "I just have to, no way around it, sorry." Assure her you are on her side in this and wish to work things out in a way that is okay with her. Instead of lecturing her on why she should report it, ask her why it is such an upsetting thing to consider and assure her that you hear her. "So you are afraid to have your name come up in this, right? What would be so bad about that?" If she said "everyone would know it was me and call me a snitch," respond by saying "yeah, I can see why that would be bad, I don't want that to happen either. What are our options?" Hopefully she has some ideas to brainstorm and you can work from there.

If not, or to supplement them, ask her if there is a teacher or guidance counselor that she trusts that she could approach. Often, if a trusted teacher or counselor is told that a student witnessed bullying but needs to know that a report must be kept confidential, this teacher can be a reliable resource to let the student/parent know if this is possible. School policy may dictate this, and finding this out is a great place to start. If you had a child in day care, you may remember that if your child was bitten or hit, many centers would not divulge the name of the aggressor. So even for the toddler set, schools often recognize when it is appropriate or not to include names in reports.

If the school assures you that your daughter's name will not be included in a report, this may convince her to go ahead and make the report herself. And ideally, the staff person will commend her for coming forward, thus making it a positive experience. You may also wish to give your daughter permission in advance to throw the school under the bus should her name somehow come out. Let her know that if someone says they heard she was the one who reported an incident, she should feel free to say that they knew she had seen something and just asked her about it. I don't ever encourage lying, but in cases like these, I always tell Kendall she is old enough to understand the difference between an outright lie and this type of lie that will allow her to save face and not become a victim herself.

If the school says they cannot guarantee confidentiality in these cases, or that the parents of the victim or bully have the right to know all of the names and facts, or if your daughter simply does not trust the school's ability to keep her name out of it, you need to go another route. Perhaps send an anonymous note to the school. To be honest, this option always bugs me. It feels so sneaky and cowardly, and I just don't like that feeling. But if the alternative is leaving a bullying situation unreported, then it is a perfectly acceptable last resort. Additionally, you may consider letting the victim's parent(s) know. This can be quite the powder keg, especially if you do not know the parents well or if you are not on good terms with them. A simple e-mail that says something like "I heard that Julie had a hard time today at recess, Kendall saw what happened, if you need any information about it please don't hesitate to call or e-mail me."

If I had to pick one aspect of bullying response to promote, it would be empowering the bystander. It would be great if parents were able to raise children who didn't become bullies, but that is trying to control something outside of ourselves and our control. And it would be great if all children were confident enough to know how to stop a bully, but again, this requires changing other people. When a bully loses his or her audience and ability to continue bullying, and those in charge address it immediately, things begin to change. Bullying thrives in a culture of silence and inaction; we need to all become a part of changing that.

The next chapter covers more on specifically what to do if your daughter is being bullied, and then we'll look at cyberbullying. Since bullying is a two-chapter endeavor, Kendall's corner makes its appearance at the end of the topic.

Chapter 7
More on Bullying

If Your Tween Is Being Bullied

If you become aware that your daughter is being bullied, you know the sense of sadness, anger, and helplessness that comes with this knowledge. In addition to the heartbreak felt at seeing your tween hurt, it can be so frustrating to find help for her to resolve the problem. There are things you can do to recognize if your daughter is being bullied, maximize a positive outcome, and help her through this.

Perhaps your daughter has been telling you about an ongoing situation at school and you have already identified that she is being bullied. Perhaps you were even able to confirm this after reading the last chapter and deciphering between bullying and conflict. There are signs that your child is being bullied to watch for, especially if she hasn't disclosed information to you. They are (20):

- Unexplained injuries
- Frequent complaints of illness or not feeling well, with or without obvious symptoms
- Missing or damaged personal property – books, clothing, etc.
- Changes in eating habits – not feeling hungry or coming home extra hungry
- Avoidance of social situations

- Decreased self esteem
- Not wanting to go to school or declining school performance
- Difficulty sleeping
- Self-destructive behaviors or suicidal comments

If your tween is exhibiting some of these signs, you should investigate further. I have talked about ways to engage your tween in conversations without being confrontational or overbearing, use those techniques to encourage her to share her problem with you. Assure her that you won't freak out and are here to help her with this issue, not makes things worse for her. Do NOT promise her that you will not tell anyone else about whatever she tells you. If this is a serious situation, you may not (and should not) keep this to yourself, and breaking this promise could be devastating to the trust between you.

If she is unwilling to tell you what is going on but you have noticed some of the above signs, or just have a gut feeling, contact her school, coach, etc. Describe what you have noticed, and ask that a counselor, teacher, or coach observe your daughter while she is with other kids to find out what might be going on. The parents of Kendall's friends are aware that she shares the details of her day fairly regularly (this is how I know that Cole got in trouble for saying the 's' word in class, Carly's mom gives her THREE cookies in her lunch, her math teacher had a big fight with her husband last weekend, and Hailey's parents are having money trouble). On more than one occasion, I have had a parent call me to tell me about their child having a problem at school, but he/she won't talk about it. They have outright asked or subtly wondered if Kendall might be able to shed some light on the situation.

I love that these parents reached out to someone they thought could help, and luckily Kendall often could. Just being able to identify which child(ren) appeared to be a part of the situation was immensely helpful, because again, this information could be brought to the attention of teachers or others who could be specific in their observations of the problem. My point is keep digging, don't let things get worse or be left unresolved.

Whether you find out that your tween is being bullied because she disclosed the information to you, or you found out through teachers or other staff and adults involved with her, and you confirmed that it is indeed bullying, it is time to take action.

First and foremost, assure her that this is not her fault, and that you are there to help her get through this and make sure the bullying stops. She needs to know that you are on her side without judgment no matter what. You will be there to help talk with her school, support her in knowing what to do and acting on it, and you will be there to make her feel loved and protected.

Ask, don't assume. Ask what is happening, and how often. A reluctant tween is not going to be a very willing participant in giving a blow by blow account, so don't worry about every detail as if she were testifying in court. But do get the general scope of what is happening, when, and how often. When talking to the school or other authority figures, more details may be needed. But for your role as parent, you are supposed to be the ally, remember?

Once you know the story, it is tempting to jump into telling her what to do. We spoke about this before regarding friendships. Don't forget that this may be new information to you, but it is not to her. Tell her how sorry you are that this is happening, and ask her what she has done when the bullying has occurred, or at least what she has wanted to do or thought that she should do. This will give you insight into what her natural reactions are under stressful circumstances as well as an indication of how she views what is happening. You may discover that she feels like she deserves it, or that it is no big deal, or that she is powerless to stop it. The more open you are in discussing the situation, the more likely you are to learn some important information that may help you help her.

Next, you need to provide her with some tools to appropriately deal with her bully. In discussing the situation with her, you may have discovered what she wishes she could do or is afraid to do when she is being bullied. This may or may not be a surprise to you based on what you already knew about her personality. Regardless, this is where to start. As I mention this yet again, I will tell you that I cannot overstate the importance of working *with* your tween's personality, not against it. Do not insist that a quiet tween stand up in the middle of the lunchroom and speak loudly to a person who terrifies them.

Ask your tween what she would feel comfortable saying and doing when/if the bully approaches her in the coming days. Gently remind her that doing nothing is not an option, that if she does not take some kind of action, the bullying is likely to continue. Can she work on making eye contact with the bully and saying "leave me alone?" Can she walk away? Brainstorm phrases and statements that feel comfortable for her, and practice saying them with conviction. Seriously, practice.

One suggestion to avoid is telling your tween to ignore the bully; walking away is different than staying in the presence of the bully. Not only is sitting and 'taking it' humiliating and sometimes scary, it will not stop the behavior. Additionally, do not suggest that she become physical. Besides the possibility of injury, she could be suspended or expelled. Even in self-defense, hearsay and re-telling the story to school personnel never come out accurately.

Working With the School or Organization

Almost every school or organization will have a policy regarding bullying. Check your specific school or organization's website as a starting point. Kendall's school simply includes a line in the handbook that says "fighting, bullying, or intimidation of any kind will not be tolerated." A bigger local school district includes information about what bullying looks like on their website, along with resources from different local and national organizations. The website also encourages students to immediately report bullying to teachers, counselors, or the principal.

Some schools, districts, or organizations may even lay out specific polices on bullying and what the procedure and consequences of bullying investigations will be. Start by doing your homework from this end – look at your student handbook, school/district website, or organizational handbooks to find out what bullying policies are in place. During a time of frustration and helplessness, this is a great way to set the foundation for you that the school or organization does not want the bullying to take place either, and that you can and should expect their help in resolving the situation. For the sake of simplicity, I will write about working with a school, but you could easily interchange school for Girl Scouts, or teacher for coach, etc. – the basic format remains the same.

The first step in working with the school is to e-mail the teacher and cc the school counselor and principal. The teacher is in closest proximity to your daughter and the problem, and I believe in working at the root of the problem. The principal is likely to direct the problem back to the teacher anyway (at least initially), so bypassing the teacher will only serve to make him/her feel that you don't have faith in his/her ability to manage the classroom. Working with the teacher is your best bet, however, I also feel that involving a counselor or principal sets the tone that you are serious, and expect results. Again, the school may have their own procedures in these cases. I would work with the procedures, but would expect that even if the counselor or principal only received cc's or written reports of what is going on, they should be informed and aware.

In your e-mail, inform the teacher that you are concerned about an issue between your child and another child(ren) in the class/school and that you would like to set up a meeting to discuss the situation. I would state that in the meeting, you would like to discuss what you have seen or heard, what impressions or observations the teacher has about the situation, what the school intends to do to explore and resolve the situation, and how you can work together to ensure a positive outcome. Through this chapter, you have already learned to take a deep breath and center yourself at the possibility that your daughter is being bullied. Sending this initial e-mail should help you to feel that you are going into a meeting feeling empowered and level-headed, not running into the school hot-headed and irrational. This also sets a tone with the school that you intend to work with them to resolve this issue, but that you expect results and their support.

I have a friend whose daughter, Emma, was having issues with a few other children in her class. I had heard stories of the goings on in this school for years before this – nothing terribly bad or out of the ordinary, but I am fascinated by what happens at other schools. I remember her telling me about the prior year, when some girl or girls in Emma's class kept shoving so much toilet paper in the toilets that they would often overflow. The consequence was that the entire class had to miss recess until someone confessed or was called out for the behavior. So fast forward one year, Emma's teacher had each child draw something on a piece of paper and put their name up top. The idea was that they would all pass these papers around and as it stopped at each child, that child would think about the name on top and write something nice about that person before passing it on. Unfortunately, someone wrote "you are ugly and stupid" on

Emma's. Even worse, the paper kept getting passed around so that some of the children who saw what was written would laugh and snicker. It was awful. Finally one brave girl (the empowered bystander!!) stopped what she was doing and brought it up to the teacher. But much of the damage was already done.

Now imagine, I'm talking on the phone with Emma's mom listening to this story maybe a week after it happened, and I'm heartbroken for Emma. I ask her what happened, and she said the teacher was mad and yelled at the class and "whoever" did this, and that was that. I often wonder if I was not focused enough on this phone call, or thinking one step ahead. Because I absent-mindedly say "isn't this the same class who had to miss recess for a week because of a toilet problem? But *THIS* happens to Emma and they scold no one in particular and send them on their way?" The next thing I hear is five seconds of silence, followed by "I gotta go," and a click. Yes, Emma's mom, who had been talking to me in her car, turned around action-movie style and drove straight to the school.

She should have been mad, her daughter deserved something more, and I applaud her advocating for her daughter. But did she take her deep breath and feel centered? Did she set a tone of cooperation and expectation with the school? I think you know the answers to these questions. She went with a full head of steam into the school and demanded action. She got a too-much-time-has-passed explanation, but the assistant principal did go into the classroom and tell the children why that wasn't nice, and what they should have done instead. It was a bad combination of the principal being out of town, a delayed reaction, and a mom who was angry and was not open to a normal course of action. I hate to use this example because I feel that the spontaneous reaction of Emma's mom was totally my fault. Of course I did not know she was headed back there, or I would have called back and tried to tell her what I am telling you before letting her go to the school.

Having this 'what not to do' story as a backdrop, realize that whether the school is awesome at responding to bullying or lacks helpful policies, a nasty attitude on your part will only sabotage your goal of helping your daughter. Go into the meeting with the intention of working with the school and maintaining your cool, and you will be surprised how much better things go. You want the focus of the school's attention on the situation, not on defusing you.

The school may have a process for the itinerary of the meeting, and that is fine. Work with them to answer their questions, provide details, and ask questions as you go. Whether following their agenda or following your own, the basic format should involve giving the details of what is occurring, asking for the school's plan to intervene and ensure your daughter's safety and well-being while at school, and asking how you can support this process. The school should be able to outline their plan in very clear terms. If possible, ask for this in writing, or at least take notes while you are there that record for you what was said.

Leave the meeting with the indication that you appreciate their careful attention to this matter, that you are available for further communication, and that in the coming weeks or months you will contact them to set up a follow-up meeting to evaluate how well the strategies worked as well as any further actions that may need to be taken. This lets them know that while you are supportive of their efforts, they will be seeing you again, and that you are expecting results and accountability.

During the time following the meeting, continue to be supportive of your daughter, echoing the message that this is not her fault, and that you are there to help her in any way she needs. And, of course, be a good listener (you had to see this one coming). Resist the urge to make the bullying the sole focus of her day. Keep her involved in her other activities and focus on the positive elements of her life. While you want her to know that you understand how upsetting the bullying is, you want her to see beyond it and that while she is dealing with a bad occurrence, there are more good things in her life.

And keep your promise of scheduling a follow up meeting with the school. Go over the changes you have noticed and heard about from your daughter or others, and ask them what they have observed and implemented as well. Talk about what might need to be continued or changed going forward. Remember, this is a process, and things may not change completely right away. If there are positive changes, continuous monitoring, and ongoing communication, then things are moving in the right direction and you are doing a great job of supporting these actions. This problem did not begin with a single action, and will not likely end with one either. Stay the course and you will ultimately see a positive change in your daughter's school experience.

You have heard some of my Kendall stories, but none of her issues have risen to the level that I needed to follow the regimen of school meetings that I describe. When she has conflicts with other students, I usually will mention something to the teacher about it. And I do so with the qualification that I want her to be aware, if she isn't already, and that if she has any feedback for me as time goes on I was open to hearing it. The only time I had to go further was when a boy that sat at Kendall's table in her fifth grade art class began saying vulgar things to her almost every day. I mentioned to the teacher that it was going on, but the behavior continued. I then called the principal and said that I was extremely uncomfortable with this boy sitting at the same table as Kendall, and that she was upset by the things he was saying. He immediately apologized that Kendall had heard these things, and said that the boy would be moved from her table for the rest of the year, and moved closer to the teacher. I sent a follow up e-mail to him, and cc'd the teacher, to thank him for his help with the situation and restate what we had talked about. I did genuinely want to thank him, but I also wanted a written record that this boy would no longer sit by Kendall.

What If Your Daughter Is the Bully

No one wants to learn that it may actually be their daughter that is the bully. Through my professional work, I have met a few honest parents who came to realize and accept that their daughter's behavior was considered bullying. I can recall only one friend who has admitted to our social circle that her child acted as a bully. More often than not, parents try to rationalize bad behavior as kids being kids, self-defense, or an isolated incident of making a bad choice. I can imagine how difficult it must be to take a hard look at what a child does and face the music that she is doing what is most hated in our schools.

You may already be concerned about your daughter's behavior, perhaps hearing problematic reports from teachers or others, or maybe you have not noticed anything abnormal going on. Regardless, if you see any of the following signs that your daughter may be bullying, it's time to take notice (21):

- Involvement in physical or verbal fights
- Having friends who bully others
- Increased aggression
- Having money or new belongings with no explanation of how they were received
- Being reprimanded or punished at school frequently
- Blaming others for her problems
- Not accepting responsibility for actions
- Often competitive and worrying about her reputation or popularity

If your daughter is bullying, there is no doubt a lot going on, more than can be adequately covered here. But know that kids don't begin bullying for no reason. You must be diligent in finding out why your daughter is bullying, which may be low self-esteem, problems at home, problems at school, or problems with peers. Start by evaluating what is going on in her life, where she is struggling, and what she is struggling with. If you are unable to find answers by talking with her and assessing her surroundings, seek help from her teacher, counselor, or other adult supervisor. Let them know that you are concerned about her behavior and possible aggression toward others and would like their feedback. And if necessary, find a therapist to help get your daughter back on track. Bottom line – do what you need to help your daughter resolve the issues that are contributing to her bullying. The hardest part may be taking a look at any family issues that are occurring, because this may mean making some tough changes of your own.

I can only imagine how difficult it is to discover that your daughter may be bullying others, and how humbling it would be to admit this to others and ask for help. But know that in doing so, you are helping your daughter to become much happier, and to learn important lessons in how to resolve problems and treat others that will carry throughout her life. You may even end up making some challenging but positive changes in your own life in the process. Find the support you need, make the changes necessary, and feel proud knowing that you met one of parenting's greatest challenges head on and did the right thing.

If there is a silver lining to the issue of bullying, it is the proliferation of information and attention given to it. I hope you found what I have written helpful, but I really do encourage you to continue to read more and keep the conversation going. If nothing else, I hope that you take away three things from my coverage of bullying. First, I hope if you were feeling panicked or unnerved by the issue of bullying, that you now feel that you have the ability to recognize it and find the help you need in a focused and rational way. Next, I hope that you instill in your daughter the responsibility to not be a silent bystander, but an empowered one who will find ways to help someone being bullied. Finally, if you find yourself needing to talk to your daughter's school or organization about bullying that she is experiencing, I want you to feel confident in advocating for her in a way that promotes a healthy relationship between you and those who you are counting on to support your daughter's well-being. In this way of 'being the change you wish to see in the world,' you will not only be setting your daughter up for success, but helping to build stronger girls and stronger communities.

In the next chapter, we'll wrap up the bullying segments with information about cyberbullying. I know this topic can feel heavy, so I wanted to give you a chance to catch your breath before moving on!

Kendall's Corner: Bullying happens everywhere. Don't think that you can keep it from happening around your kid. Even if you send your kid to a private or Christian school, you may not get the same results you were hoping for. I hate to say it, but I went from a public school to a Christian school and don't get me wrong, it's a great atmosphere, but the same amount of bullying is happening.

For the kids- you should never just watch someone get bullied, trust me, you **WILL** regret it. I do. People's lives are put in danger when they are being bullied. Bullying doesn't always mean physical. The hardest kind of bullying is emotional. People who are being bullied may be the most emotionally strong person you have ever met but when being bullied repeatedly, they most likely will lose their confidence. Some people will lose their lives because they can't take it anymore. That is up to you to stop it. You could just ignore it and when they are gone that will never leave your heart and you will know you could have saved their life. So when you see something do something. It's never *when* you are going to do something, it's *what* you are going to do.

Chapter 8
Cyberbullying

When I would work with clients in my parenting classes, it would usually go a couple of different ways. There were people who came to the classes with no clear goals or issues but wanted general parenting information, and then became a little restless when a difficult subject came up that either unexpectedly hit home or that they didn't want to face. And there were also people who came to the classes with a defined problem, and couldn't get enough of the material on that subject. Either way, it was hard to conduct the class in a way that suited everyone's needs, and at certain points I would check in with the class to acknowledge what they might be feeling in their personal parenting journey.

I mention this because I wish that I could check in with each one of you. Depending on what is going on with your tween, you probably read some chapters more intently than others. If you are overwhelmed by the topic of bullying, then you are probably emotionally drained after the last two chapters. If you are dealing with bullying with your tween or are gung ho about preventing bullying and empowering your daughter, you are hopefully feeling energized by these chapters and devouring the information. This topic does not reach everyone in the same way. How could it? We bring our own experiences to this area, and our daughters are going through these years in vastly different ways. So take a minute to check in with yourself, know that however you are receiving this information is just fine, and let's tackle one more chapter on cyberbullying.

What Is Cyberbullying

Cyberbullying takes place with the use of technology. Cell phones, computers, iPads and social networking sites all fall into this category. Mean text messages, e-mails, rumors spread via technology, embarrassing pictures, videos, or creating fake profiles are all examples of cyberbullying (22).

How Cyberbullying Is Different Than In-Person Bullying

I remember being this age, and having more than one bad day. I also remember spending evenings at home, surrounded only by my parents, brother, and sisters, or in my room. The comfortable surroundings of stuffed animals and my guinea pig reminded me that nothing from the outside world could get in, and other than arguments with my siblings about which record to play, I had a reprieve from whatever or whoever was bothering me. One difficult aspect of cyberbullying is that the victim cannot get away from it. It can happen all day and night, every day, and reach the victim in the places where they used to feel safe and secure; places like home. And victims can be by themselves when the cyberbullying occurs, making helpful bystanders and authority figures that may otherwise help unavailable in the moment. It's upsetting to think about how much this intensifies the feelings of isolation.

Also frustrating is the fact that cyberbullying can be done anonymously, making identification of the bully difficult, if not impossible. And the messages and images posted can be distributed so quickly to a very broad audience. This makes deleting inappropriate, hurtful, harassing, or embarrassing messages and images extremely difficult. As if the cyberbullying itself weren't enough, kids who are cyberbullied are more likely to (23):

- Use alcohol and drugs
- Skip school or be unwilling to attend school
- Experience in-person bullying
- Receive poor grades
- Have lower self-esteem
- Have more health problems

Frequency of Cyberbullying

I have to say that statistics on cyberbullying are constantly changing. Kids are using cell phones and social networking at earlier and earlier ages. And with so many types of communication available and new applications and sites added constantly, I don't believe there can be a number that adequately represents the occurrence of cyberbullying for very long. What samples of statistics do show is that, over time, the numbers are going up. However, it is important to be aware of the basic statistics in order to create a baseline to work from, so let's look at the numbers that are available at the time of this writing (24).

- Approximately half of young people have experienced some form of cyberbullying, and between 10 and 20 percent experience it on a regular basis.
- Mean, cruel comments and the spreading of rumors are the most common types of cyberbullying.
- Girls are at least as likely as boys to be victims or perpetrators of cyberbullying, though some research indicates that they may be more likely than boys (25).
- Less than one in five cyberbullying incidents are reported to law enforcement.
- Over half of young people do not report cyberbullying to their parents.

The numbers on how many kids are using cell phones and social media changes constantly, and new applications and devices pop up all the time. And in terms of the trends where you live, well, you know better than me how many kids are using these things and at what ages. Looking at this information from even the most conservative estimates, we know for sure that cyberbullying does happen and that it is a serious problem.

As we've discussed, girls tend to use more indirect methods to bully – spreading rumors, telling secrets, and shunning. This makes cyberbullying very attractive to girls, even some who may not otherwise be bullies. The opportunity to be mean to someone without having to even be near that person is ever-present with the online world. So once again we are left with heavy hearts, unable to keep our daughters entirely out of the way of those who would cyberbully them, and in even more distressing circumstances, out of their own way should they choose to cyberbully someone else. But similar to the previous chapters on in-person bullying, we can maximize the odds that will keep them from being a victim or perpetrator of cyberbullying.

Establish Clear Rules about Technology

When Kendall got her first phone, I thought I would be right on top of everything. I would know what sites to allow and prohibit, what rules would be beneficial, and who she was talking to at all times. Wow, was I in over my head. What I quickly learned is that things change so swiftly in the cyberworld that I could not possibly roll out one set of rules that would cover her until she leaves for college. I also learned that tweens' knowledge of technology is astounding, and mine will always lag behind. I still feel fairly confident about the way we monitor her cell phone and online behavior, it is just much more adaptive than I had imagined. I believe the best approach to establishing rules are finding ones that set positive expectations and that allow for flexibility.

First, don't imply that you are going to catch her or set a trap for her. I know many parents who have found apps or software that will snoop on their children's phones, or use GPS to catch them when they are somewhere they are not supposed to be. They seem unusually excited about the moment when they can yell "AHA!" when their child falls into the trap. I think what underlies this is the belief that catching their child will prove that they weren't duped and that they still have the upper hand. What they don't realize is that this implies to their child that they expect them to mess up. Awareness is good, suspicion is not. I don't expect to find anything bad on Kendall's phone, my message to her is that we are working together to keep her safe. With that in mind, use rules such as:

•Do not write any message that could hurt or embarrass yourself or someone else. This is true even if someone else said something bad about you.

•Do not forward any message that you see that contains something hurtful or embarrassing to yourself or someone else.

•Before visiting any website or downloading any app, please ask for permission. You may wish to keep a listed of permitted sites. (Some websites will be easy to okay, but others may require you to check them out yourself. This is the same story with apps, not to mention some are free, others cost money.)

•Do not share your password with friends. (This compromises the control they have over their information.)

•Do not take or send any pictures of yourself without.... (Decide what is appropriate for your family. Maybe you only want face shots, nothing from the neck down. Maybe no bathing suits? You get the idea, decide what fits in with your values and go from there – hey, maybe use her vision board or mission statement!)

•You must personally know everyone that you are texting. (This seems crazy to me, but it is possible to meet someone online in a game or think it is a friend-of-a-friend and then have that evolve into texting with them on personal devices. Make sure your tween can personally identify each contact at a level that is acceptable to you.)

•You may not text..... (Again, decide what's okay with you. Kendall was not allowed to text boys until eighth grade. Do you want your daughter texting boys? Teachers? Coaches? Talk about what you are okay with and set that as your expectation.)

•Consider a policy of turning phones in to mom or dad at a certain time in the evening, or before bedtime. I wish I had done this when Kendall first got her phone. At this point, I have decided that it is not a battle we will fight – I think if we gave her the choice of oxygen at night or her phone, she'd try to find a way to live without oxygen. We have not had any issues with her texting when she should be sleeping, so it would certainly feel like an unjust punishment to her. But I wish that this rule had started the day she got her phone so that she would have never known any other way, with the simple explanation that there is no reason to have access to the phone at bedtime.

•When in doubt, picture mom and dad. We use this notion for many things with Kendall. We always tell her that if she is not sure if something is okay to do, she should picture her dad or me standing over her shoulder watching what she's doing. Would she still do whatever she was about to do? This can be a great way to decide whether something is a good idea or not.

You will likely come up with other rules that fit for your family. Many schools, churches, libraries, and local police departments offer workshops on cybersafety. I recommend attending these to recognize the current trends and to learn ways to keep your daughter safe. Because things change so quickly, I recommend not attending one and then thinking you are all set. As I mentioned before, complacency is not your friend, and things will change quickly. Allow your basic rules to cover online behavior from a foundational and proactive stance, but recognize that there is value in keeping up with the latest information.

Be Aware of School Rules

This is short and sweet. Many schools and school districts have created policies regarding the use of technology both at school and off campus. Check the school's website or student handbook to make sure that you and your daughter are aware of these rules.

And as for You...

Your daughter now has some rules. You, too, need to keep some guidelines in mind for yourself in order to keep an ongoing tab on what is happening in her virtual world.

•Have an idea of what she does online and in texts. Let her know up front that you will be looking in from time to time on who she is talking to and what she's looking at. No need to burst in and ambush her, just randomly say "hey, can you show me some of your texts?" and sit down and look at them together, asking questions about what you see. If you approach this in a way that suggests more curiosity than accusation, it can be a positive way to find out more about what she is doing. If you see things that concern you, ask questions to clarify what you see, but don't freak out. For example, I saw an instance on Kendall's phone where, in a group text, a disagreement between two people escalated into the majority of the group pouncing on one person. I asked her to explain the context of the argument, but didn't say anything more right then. I later talked with her about how to handle situations that start harmless but might get out of control. She ended up using that incident as an example in our discussion.

•Make sure you know her passwords, but assure her that you aren't using them every day, you just have them in case you need them.

•Follow her on social media. Be her friend or follower on the sites she uses. And encourage others to do so as well. My sister follows Kendall on Twitter, and is more tech-savvy than I am. She has been able to let me know when she sees Kendall forwarding false information (like the fake information about a company soon to charge for this or that, and an urging to forward to as many people as possible). Even one or two extra sets of eyes can help you keep up with your daughter's activities.

•If you feel like online software or apps that track your daughter's online actions and report them to you are necessary, do not rely solely on them. Kendall's middle school issues iPads for every student. They keep a tight rein on what the kids are able to access, and what they are able to view. I listened at the parent meeting where the technology expert explained to us how multiple filters and safeguards would keep the kids from being able to access the open Internet or get on any site that the school hadn't pre-approved. That night at dinner, I was relaying this information to my husband, and Kendall said "oh yeah, Michael found a way to get into the Internet from one of the apps they installed on our iPads." If we had put all of our faith in the 'impenetrable' safeguards that the school had come up with, we would have had a false sense of security. We consistently checked what was available on this device, and found troubling content more than once.

If Your Tween Does Experience Cyberbullying

Many of the same concepts from the previous chapter on in-person bullying apply here. Hopefully through the steps above, your daughter will feel comfortable coming to you with any issues she is having. Do not lose control and take her phone or computer away; this will make her feel that she is being punished, and will reduce the chances that she will come to you in the future. Let her know that you would like to check her phone more often while this is happening so that you can help her resolve the issue.

Similar to in-person bullying, make an effort to let your daughter know that you are on her side here, and will discuss everything that you intend to do with her. This is a vulnerable time for her, and you will only make it worse by taking her by surprise by calling the perpetrators' parents or driving her to the police station. Thoughtful, well-discussed actions will make her feel that you can handle this with her and are strong enough (and stable enough!) for both of you.

Keep an accurate record of the cyberbullying. Record dates, times, and descriptions of what has occurred. Save and print screenshots, e-mails, and text messages. Ask her to not respond to or forward any cyberbullying messages, but to block the person who is cyberbullying.

Report the cyberbullying to the school. In many states, schools must address bullying or cyberbullying even when it occurs off-campus during non-school hours. And remembering that cyberbullying is often linked to in-person bullying, it is important to end this quickly. Refer to the tips in the previous chapter for working with the school in order to maximize a positive outcome.

As a side note to this, it may be helpful to know that many states have confusing or no cyberbullying laws. And imagine the system overload for those states that do: it can be difficult for the police to apply the laws, and many district attorneys are ill-equipped to handle the number of complaints that are filed. Because of this, law enforcement and the courts are currently, at least in part, looking to the schools to handle these issues. This means that it may be frustrating to find resolution to a relatively new problem that has states and the country trying to catch up with and untangle technology from the law. But it also means that schools may be the best source to resolve the situation effectively.

However, if the cyberbullying includes threats of violence, child pornography or sexually explicit messages or photos, hate crimes, or taking photos or videos of someone in a place where privacy would be expected, these are absolutely worthy of a report to local law enforcement. If you are unsure of what to report, you may wish to call the police station and ask them if filing a report is possible and what will be involved, as well as what the implications of filing one will be. I'm certainly not trying to talk you out of getting law enforcement involved, in some cases it may be wise to have something on file. I'm just asking you to consider all of your options and what you are looking to accomplish with each action you take.

Cyberbullying may violate the terms of service of social media sites or Internet service providers. Visiting these sites can alert you to what is considered inappropriate and you may wish to report the cyberbullying to the site so that they can handle the offender on their end. It also helps them to track this problem, and will help inform future policies and procedures. Visiting the site will also allow you to learn how to maximize the safety of your daughter's account by controlling who can contact her or view her profile, and can allow you to block certain users.

What I hope you take away from this chapter is the awareness that cyberbullying happens at any time, day or night, and can reach your daughter in the safety of her own home. Also, with the increased use of devices and social media, cyberbullying is likely to expand while parents and schools try to keep up with the latest in technology trends. No single approach is sufficient in contending with this issue; managing your daughter's virtual activities through conversations, attentiveness, and ongoing education will keep you well informed and in the best possible position to handle whatever situation arises.

Kendall's Corner: I know that it is important to know about cyberbullying, but I have to admit it is definitely not topping my priorities. There is a lot of bantering on the social media sites that I use, but I usually think that is not anything to report. I do know that if I see something that is going to affect someone, I am going to for sure say something to my mom.

I also know that my mom checks my texts, she asks to see my phone or have me show her what's going on in my cyber-world. It doesn't bug me because it's not all the time, and she doesn't try to make it sneaky, and she doesn't assume I am doing anything bad. I know she is just keeping an eye on me. If you make sure your child tells someone that they are being cyberbullied and you make sure she steps in when people are getting hurt, she will be okay. I remember what my mom tells me about cyberbullying and not being a part of the problem, so it's important to tell your daughter about it, I just don't want you to think that she is making cyberbullying her top priority and that she is super excited about finding and stopping it.

Chapter 9
Drugs and Alcohol

I can personally attribute many lost hours of sleep and the consumption of countless chips and cookies to the issue of under-age drug and alcohol use. The sentiments expressed by friends and parents that I know range from denial that this is even an issue to address during the tween years to those who are convinced that their child is going to go from fifth grade straight into rehab. The best parenting practice, as evidenced by research, is that we need to be talking about this with our tweens – early and often.

Your daughter is in the perfect storm of growing up, she is beginning to think you may not know everything, she is starting to think her friends do know everything, and she is inundated with shows and songs that glorify drinking and drug use. And don't even get me started about the under-age celebrities who are frequently caught drinking or doing drugs that rarely seem to face consequences and post less than contrite messages about their antics. This sometimes appears to be such an uphill battle, but I am here to tell you that you are still the one that can have the biggest impact on your daughter in this area. Let's start with a reality check, and then talk about what you can do to keep your daughter away from the pressures of drugs and alcohol.

Every day, an average of 8,120 people twelve years old and older try drugs for the first time, and 12,800 try alcohol.

Since 2008, marijuana use among teenagers has increased 21 percent. And daily marijuana use among high-school seniors is at a thirty year high (no pun intended). More than 40 percent of college students binge drink (having five or more drinks at a time). The abuse of prescription pills is growing at an alarming rate, with deaths resulting from overdose keeping a chilling pace (26). As with any gauge of social issues, sources vary in their reporting. But no matter which source you go to, the numbers of young people drinking and using drugs is scary and cannot be ignored.

Trying to guard our children against this influence is made so much more difficult by the fact that our culture seems to celebrate substance use. Music, for example, often references excessive drinking as fun and trendy, even featuring brand names in songs. A 2013 study found that when drinking is mentioned in a popular song, it is almost always portrayed in a positive way (27). More troubling are the findings of many long-term studies which indicate that exposing young people to alcohol marketing in mass media increases the likelihood that they will start or increase their drinking (28). We were already mad at popular music back in chapter three because of the crude lyrics, so this just intensifies our urge to grab the radio dial.

Because drug and alcohol use most often begins during the tween and teen years (the median age for initial drug use is 14), most prevention efforts have logically been tailored to them. Despite this, the attitudes about drugs and alcohol are actually becoming more positive than in the past (29). A study conducted by The Partnership at Drugfree.org (30) showed a growing belief in the acceptability of drug use and drinking. Besides reporting a drop in the number of teenagers who would not want to hang around drug users, there was an increase in those who believe that being high felt good and who report that friends usually get high at parties. In this study, almost half of teens reported that they didn't see a big risk associated with heavy daily drinking, and only a third strongly disapproved of their friends getting drunk. When it comes to prescription drug abuse, the study revealed that one in four teenagers admits abusing or misusing a prescription drug not prescribed for them, and of those, twenty percent had done so before the age of fourteen. Over and over, we see studies and surveys that ask tweens and teens what the biggest influence is regarding their decision to drink or use drugs. Repeatedly, the result is always the same: parents. Research has shown that kids who learn about the risks of drugs from their parents are up to 50 percent less likely to use drugs. Despite this, only 37 percent of kids report learning about these risks from their parents (31). The eye-rolling and groans may suggest otherwise, but your daughter really does hear what you are saying! During the tween years, there are some guidelines to keep in mind that will help you know what to say and do to keep her making safe and healthy decisions.

Make Sure She Knows Your Rules and Expectations

This seems obvious, but this matter may be less black and white to your daughter than you think. When Kendall was in sixth grade, her classmates were talking about whether or not they had tried alcohol. Many said they had tried a sip of mom or dad's drink at one time or another, and a few said they were allowed sips of champagne at a special occasion. I asked Kendall what she said, and she told me that she said she was never allowed to have even a sip, and never would be until she was 21. We have always been crystal clear on this point. I don't even let her carry drinks to adults, that has always been a pet peeve of mine. It makes me cringe when adults ask kids to deliver bottles of beer or other alcohol to themselves or to guests.

If your rules and expectations are that drinking or drugs of any kind are unacceptable to use, you need to say it, and say it clearly. This means not as a one-time thing, not just a little, not if a parent says it's okay, and not if a friend tells her it's no big deal. It is never okay with you and never will be. We may have always said no to Kendall when others were toasting with champagne, etc., but had we never clearly stated our values and expectations around alcohol, she could have been confused when she heard her friends talking about trying alcohol.

Start by defining what you mean by drinking and drugs. Make sure to include alcohol of any kind, smoking cigarettes, e-cigarettes, marijuana, synthetic marijuana – basically anything that is smoked is included. Additionally, any street drugs, over the counter, or prescription drugs should be included. And finally, any household items used to get high as well, such as paint, gasoline, and aerosol items used as inhalants.

It seems that by the time adults have figured out the latest trend in drug use, kids are already on to the next thing. Because of this, I believe it is important to keep current on dangerous trends, but it's more important to be proactive with your tween. Give her the basics of what is considered a drug or alcohol, but give her tools to be able to judge for herself something new that may come up without you knowing. I often explain to Kendall that anything used for something other than the intended use is not okay. It's not okay to use cough medicine without a parent's permission and when you are not sick, it's not okay to sniff nail polish remover, etc.

Additionally, I warned her about key phrases she would likely hear from someone offering her something dangerous. Anytime someone says "try this, it will make you feel funny/weird/happy/spacey" it is also not okay to try. Bottom line is that anything that is used to make you feel something other than normal is a bad idea and not okay to try. Providing this information as a backdrop allows her to know that if someone offers her something, even if it is something you hadn't mentioned to her, she will have the awareness that something is not right.

Role Play Scenarios

When I picture you reading 'role play' for the fifth or sixth time in this book, I have to smile a little because I know some of you said "you've got to be kidding me." Believe me, if I didn't know how effective role plays are for tweens, I wouldn't keep suggesting them. There is simply no substitute for increasing her comfort level in facing certain situations.

She is not likely to be approached by a stranger offering her cocaine in an alley. But it's completely possible that she will be with or around kids who are giving out ADHD medication at recess, or girls who want to try the alcohol they found during a sleepover. Practice these kinds of scenarios. Provide your tween with ways to say no, and ways to remove herself from the situation. Stress that she can always use you as her excuse, it's a free pass to blame you for something! A variety of responses is good to have in her arsenal. It's always great if she is able to simply say "I think doing this sounds lame, I'm not going to try it," and it's a good idea to practice confident replies like this. However, tweens are not going to always feel confident, so make sure she has some replies that simply let her off the hook without taking a stand. "If my mom found out, she would ground me for a year!" or "I have to spend the whole night with my parents right in my face, so they would totally know if I did this." As with other role plays, brainstorm ideas with your tween so that she comes up with ideas that resonate with her and that she knows she would be comfortable saying.

Beyond this, make sure she knows that if the kids she is with are going to be trying drugs or alcohol, she needs to find a way to leave that location. If she has a cell phone, it's as easy as texting you to tell you she needs to get out of there. You can have a pre-understood agreement that if she texts and asks you to call or text her and tell her to come home, you will do just that and ask questions later. If she does not have a cell phone, she can come up with a number of reasons to call you or say that she needs to leave: she forgot she has an appointment or lesson, she forgot she has homework to do, she has plans with the family, she is not feeling well, and anything else you and her may come up with.

Avoid the temptation to declare that if her friends are involved in these kinds of activities, she will never see them again. As we've discussed, the thought of losing her social circle will likely freak her out and possibly keep her from telling you what is really going on in her world. For the purposes of role playing and keeping her out of harm's way, you just need to focus on what she will say and do in the moment.

Know Who She Spends Time with (or as Kendall Says "Be All up in Her Business")

The more you know about who your daughter's friends are and how they spend their time, the better off you will be. Not only does this let your daughter know that you are never more than a few steps away when she's at your home with a friend, it lets her know that you are likely to find out what goes on during phone calls, cell phone exchanges, and in-person time spent hanging out. This does not mean that you should inundate her and her friends with questions, this just means that you should demonstrate a healthy presence in her life.

When this topic comes up with my friends, I often hear the worry that soon enough our daughters will encounter friends or peers who are drinking or doing drugs. Frequently I hear the rationalization that just because our daughter's friend drinks or uses drugs, doesn't mean our daughter will. In fact, maybe our daughter will be the good influence that convinces the friend to stop this behavior. I'm the big downer for them, and if you have the same thoughts, allow me to be the downer for you: it doesn't work like that. Of course there are exceptions, and it is always possible that if one friend has lost her way and is vulnerable to peer pressure to try something dangerous, the other better-adjusted friend may be able to talk her out of it. I never say never. But unfortunately, having friends who try drugs or alcohol is absolutely a big risk factor for tweens and teens trying drugs or alcohol (32).

Here is another instance in which I believe that you know your daughter best and can make the best judgment call regarding how being a healthy presence will look with your tween. If, for whatever reason, you have not spoken much with your daughter's friends and their parents in earlier years, it might seem strange to suddenly be calling other moms and being involved with your daughter's friends. Approach this in a way that will not send your daughter running in the other direction. This is important, and you need to find a way to raise your level of awareness, so keep at it even if you are a little uncomfortable at first.

If you have always demonstrated a level of participation with your tween's friends and their parents, this should not change much. You may find that your daughter becomes more annoyed with your interest, requiring a little more finesse on your part, so as not to embarrass her by daring to ask her friend what activities she is involved in at the moment ("*mom*! Stop being so *weird!*"). I have always been a bit nosy, er, involved when it comes to the people Kendall is around. I am the mom who drops Kendall off at play dates by going to the door and asking if there are guns in the house, would anyone else be coming over, what video games were allowed, has your house been checked for asbestos, could I have a floor plan of your house, etc. Okay, the last two never happened, that was what my husband joked that he imagined was in my litany of questions.

If you are able to volunteer at your daughter's school (or Girl Scout troop or church group, etc.), that is a fabulous way to get a first-hand look at what the kids that she interacts with are like. You may be able to meet other parents this way as well. Work schedules and other commitments may make this impossible, but there are other ways to be involved. Offer to arrange an outing with your daughter and her friends, to the movies, bowling, or another activity. No need to insert yourself in their conversations – making sure you are there the whole time, you can be a fly on the wall. You'll be surprised what they talk about when they think you are not paying attention. Invite the other moms to stay for coffee during the play dates, or ask if they want to walk around the mall with you while you follow the girls. Use this time to get a sense of what their concerns are with this peer group, and what things they are talking about with their daughters.

Kendall is generally okay with me being around her and her friends. But she has increasingly wanted some space, asking me if her and her friends can just hang out alone in her room, the play room, or backyard. No problem. I am the queen of finding reasons to pop in: "here's a snack girls"... "do your moms know what time to pick you up"... "let me get those dishes out of your way"... "weird, the tv upstairs isn't working, is this one fine? Oh good." You get the idea, get involved.

Separate Fact from Fiction

Kids are exposed to numerous messages of drug and alcohol use in the media. Short of unplugging everything, we cannot get away from these images and messages. When watching a television show or movie with your tween, ask open-ended questions and find out what they think. When a program makes being drunk or high look funny and trendy, point that out. If their favorite celebrities or characters are using drugs or alcohol, you won't get very far just saying how lame that really is. She is likely to think that some of these people are cool, and is not willing to dislike them for their behavior. You could not have convinced me in the 80s that anything Jon Bon Jovi or the Fresh Prince of Bel Air did was uncool. It takes finding the differences in what is portrayed and what is applicable to your tween's real life. Acknowledge that what they are seeing in the media makes drinking and drugs look like the cool and popular thing to do. But break it down a bit. "Do you think those girls could really get drunk in her room and go unnoticed? And knowing how sick they are going to be soon, do you think she'd be able to get up for track practice early the next morning? What do you think her coach would say when he found out?"

Asking your tween what she thinks of what she sees can help build a bridge between you, and take some of the heat off of her. If you are able to tolerate her thinking that the latest young star going off the deep end is cool, you are showing her that you understand her world. "I can see why you think her life is amazing, she drives that awesome car, has tons of money, and is out dancing all the time looking really pretty. But what's the down side of her life? What would make her choices the wrong choices for you?" I twitch a little when I have to say the name Justin Bieber out loud. And luckily Kendall is not a true "Belieber." But she does go through phases where she thinks he's pretty cool. I have to acknowledge the reasons she finds him appealing (more twitching). Sometimes I just say "yep, his car is pretty neat," and leave it at that. And then when we see clips of him doing sobriety tests at the police station, I say "wow, that's too bad. But he is just able to pay people to get him out of jail, and he doesn't have school or his family to get back to so I don't think he really cares. What do you think dad's face would look like arriving at the police station for you?" Ah, look who's twitching now.

One of the sayings in our family is "if you can't be a good example, you'll serve as a horrible warning." We don't sugar-coat a lot of behavior, from celebrities and even members of our families. When a celebrity tragically dies of an overdose, we talk about it – not as a 'isn't that an anomaly' kind of thing, but a 'that's the risk of doing drugs, this person did not *want* to die but they were not able to stop doing drugs.' Sadly, these stories are good conversation starters. Ask your tween what she thinks about what happened, and the reality that this person likely started taking drugs because it was the thing to do, and that even had they wanted to stop, they were obviously unable to do so. Not starting at all would have saved this life. The level of depth that you go into depends on your tween's personality as well as her age. With younger, more sensitive tweens, you may only wish to cover the basics of the story, while older tweens may be able to handle more details and depth. You want to address the topic, but this does not need to be a scared straight program either.

Kids Are More Likely to Do What You Do than What You Say

We'd all like to believe that kids don't pick up on some of the things that we do. I have a serious fear of bees (ridiculous may be a better word, but whatever); despite knowing better, I jump, scream, and run when one gets near me. Since Kendall was little, I have told her that the best thing to do when a bee gets near her is to sit still and it will eventually go away. What do you think she does when a bee approaches? She jumps, screams, and runs. She does know better, right? I've *told* her what to do, but she does what I *do*, not what I *say*. This is a silly example that illustrates a serious point.

As you might imagine, I get asked a lot of parenting questions by friends and people that I meet. Sometimes I have to ask people "do you want me to answer this as a friend or as a psychologist," because the answers are often different. When our kids were smaller, people would ask me about negative behaviors that their child was exhibiting. As a friend, I would probably say "wow, you DO have the most difficult child in the whole school" or "you poor thing, I'm sure this phase will pass." But as a psychologist, I would be more likely to say "he's acting out because he has no structure or stability in his day."

I have been faced most often with this dilemma when people ask me about alcohol use by parents. Like so many of you, the people that I socialize with enjoy wine or beer with dinner, or drinks when out with friends. This is not necessarily a problem; there is a way to demonstrate responsible drinking. But I will say this in all seriousness: your tween has learned how to drink long before she ever takes a sip. Here's how:

•She knows why she should drink – maybe it's to combat stress, or if she has had a bad day, or because she's out to dinner, or because she's sitting down to watch tv.

•She knows when she should drink – has she seen that this is what people do when they get home at the end of the day, or because it's what friends do when they get together, or because it's 8:00?

•She knows how she should drink – one drink in her hand before she even sets down her purse after coming home, one glass of wine with dinner every night, more bottles than she can count during a party, or as many beers as it takes to get from being a ball of stress to a couch potato.

•She knows how she should feel about drinking – she knows if it is something to be ashamed of and done as secretively as possible, if it is done as a habit without giving it a second thought, or if it is something entertaining and something to brag about because she's heard so many 'funny' stories about people she knows being drunk.

When it's put like this, I think fear is struck in the hearts of all who suddenly see a tape reel of their drinking history, problematic or not. We suddenly realize what our tweens have been exposed to by us or those around us. I am not here to judge how much you should or should not be drinking. But I have found that a lot of parents downplay the impact that they believe their drinking has had on their children, or insist that despite their actions, they have told their children not to drink and believe this is sufficient.

There is a significant amount of research that concludes that children who grow up in a home in which one or both parents drink alcohol are at greater risk of beginning to drink and drinking excessively (33). This research extends to tobacco use as well. In fact, parents who smoked at the time their children were in the third grade had children who were 64 percent more likely to smoke by the time they reached their senior year in high school (34).

No lecture here, but a suggestion to take a good, hard look at the drinking habits of your family and friends. If there are unhealthy messages being sent to your tween, you probably already knew this but may have been hesitant to make any difficult changes. Please hear my psychologist take on this, not my friend take. Take this opportunity to make the changes you need to make. And feel free to switch the word alcohol to Xanax, cigarettes, or marijuana. You get the idea – don't kid yourself.

As far as what you should be doing to model responsible drinking, make sure that you:

•Never drink and drive

•Have plenty of times where you opt for something other than alcohol to drink

•Don't make drinking look glamorous, and challenge those who do

•Talk about ways other than drinking to deal with stress

•If you are with a group that is drinking excessively, leave the situation and tell your tween that you are leaving because you don't approve of what is going on

You need to ask yourself how you expect your tween to behave around alcohol. And then ask yourself how much of that she has seen modeled for her. Children have a hard time becoming something they have never seen.

Many of the statistics and research in the area of drug and alcohol use pertains more to teens than tweens, it is much easier to find information relating to teens. I included it because our tweens are peeking around the corner at this problem. And because of what they are subjected to now, the foundation is being set for how they will handle it. Take a fresh, objective look at the world around your tween. Find out what she is hearing and talking about with her friends in a way that opens up or broadens communication on this topic. Define and explain your expectations for her regarding all manner of substances, but do so in a way that lets her know that you are approachable about the topic. Having a realistic view of what exists in her daily life, and working with her to increase her comfort level in avoiding and dealing with problems will allow you both to navigate the waters ahead with confidence rather than alarm.

Kendall's Corner: Drugs and alcohol are bad for you. I know this because my parents tell me about it over and over...and over and over! That is a good thing though, you can never say enough how bad drugs and under-age drinking are. I am so glad my parents taught me about this early because now when my friends are talking about drinking and how fun it seems, I know that it isn't really fun because I know that I will get sick and I know that drugs and drinking are bad. It was confusing at first, to think that drugs and drinking are bad, but then hear friends who I think are good kids talking about it. But I just need to remember what I know to be true – this makes it less confusing.

Chapter 10
Something Bright and Sunny!

I debated the need to add this chapter. But when I proudly submitted the chapter on things that influence tweens and how to avoid negative influences to my editor, I excitedly asked him if he liked it, to which he replied "NO." What followed was a (polite) rant about how it sounds as if the world is out to get tweens and how there is apparently nothing fun or appropriate for them to do. I could certainly see his point, and that ended my debate. I wanted to make sure to include this chapter to emphasize what I hope you already know: the tween years can be a fun and happy time.

A lot of what I ask you to do in this book can be reduced to one theme – involvement. I am unwavering in my belief that being appropriately involved in your daughter's life will repair, maintain, or create a positive relationship and will bolster her confidence and self esteem. And despite the concerns that require your involvement in an "I'll save you from the world" kind of way, there is such an opportunity for involvement to be fun, silly, and light.

Connections that Count

I can't believe that I'm about to follow the phrase 'fun, silly, and light' with the word research, but I just can't help myself. I know I have already asked you to make a big commitment to taking on any subjects in the book where you feel you and your tween need improvement or extra attention. I know you are probably very busy with a job, relationships, other children, insert additional time-suckers here. More than just broadly saying "remember to have fun, okay," I want to really hammer this point home, which is why I will tell you that research backs me up. Recent studies have shown that the social and intellectual development of preadolescent children can be improved and deepened when they are exposed to regular and appropriate use of humor and laughter, by parents and/or teachers (35).

Beyond merely the belief that laughter is the best medicine, the concept of fun and humor allows for another angle from which to approach a connection with your tween. We want them to connect with us when they are sad, when they need our guidance, and when they need our protection and support. We can add another layer of connection simply by laughing together and having fun and light-hearted moments. You certainly don't need me to explain what fun is to you, but I do want to offer you a broad range of reminders and suggestions. My guess is that as you read them you will say either "we used to do that – I don't know why we stopped," or "we already do this," or (dare I hope) "great idea!"

Do Things You Already Know You Like

Do you remember how much fun it was to be in control of your daughter's activities when she was younger? I loved planning what fun thing we did for the day, or what activity Kendall would try. Wouldn't she look cute in a tutu? Let's try ballet. I wanted her to develop more confidence and be able to speak up for herself, so I signed her up for tae kwon do. When I didn't care for the behavior of the child down the street I simply removed his name from our vocabulary and she quickly forgot he existed. Of course Kendall had her own opinions about things, and expressed enjoyment in certain activities and displeasure in others. But by and large, I was the ringmaster of our family circus.

Perhaps I was reluctant to give up this power, but it was hard when she entered the tween years and developed more interests of her own. A large part of this evolves naturally: she begins to hear about what friends are interested in and because of the desire to relate to peers, she wants to try some new things that they are talking about. Or other kids may deem various interests as cool or uncool, making her want to start or stop something she has previously done. And depending on how many children you have, you may already be knee-deep in activities, so changing things up may throw you and your schedule into a tailspin.

Kendall has always been involved in sports. She is a very social kid and loves the team culture – to this day her favorite part of any sport she plays is the time she gets to spend with the other girls. Growing up in our home with a father who played football throughout high school, college and beyond, she was destined to love or at least endure watching football on Sundays. Luckily, she loves it, and even knew the referees' hand signals by the time she was three (her dad's doing, and a popular party trick for her). So sports has been a constant in our home, as both something we have always enjoyed doing as a family, and something that changes as she refines her interest in particular sports.

There are pros and cons to these changes. It's great to try new things and develop new interests. Of course, it's important to make sure she doesn't want to try something new in order to fit in or gain popularity. And similarly, you don't want her to give up something she loves just because someone finds it uncool. Kendall did not want to try the local cotillion – fine. She did want to try soccer – great. We mutually agreed that she would not quit piano. And the mutual agreement I'm referring to is her dad and me, but whatever, she remained in piano.

My point here is that I tried very hard to keep up with and support her new interests, while preserving a few that we weren't ready to let go of. This led to feelings of disconnectedness, which is when I realized that even though she was starting to increase the time spent with other people and new activities, I could still rely on the basics to connect with her. She has always loved to cook, so I made sure we spent some time in the kitchen together. And we have always enjoyed family walks, even just around the block, so we made sure to work in a few laps a couple of times a week. You get the idea; take an interest in the new things that your daughter is discovering, but don't forget to hang onto some of the fundamentals that bring you enjoyment.

Have Ongoing Projects

Whether you have discovered something new that you enjoy doing together, or you are maintaining a previous hobby, have something ongoing that is an easy go-to project when you have some down time together. Scrapbooking, sewing, knitting, crafting, or an ongoing game of chess – things like this can be worked on in limited amounts of time, and started and stopped as needed. You can choose something that the whole family can work on (or whoever is home at the moment) or something that gives you some one on one time with your tween. Check out sites like Pinterest if you need some inspiration.

Read Together

Reading to or with kids is one of my absolute favorite things to do. Bedtime stories or just cuddling up to read is very high on my list. In fact, I love it so much that even as Kendall started getting older, I never stopped. True, she began refusing to sit on my lap, but we adapted. We read her favorite chapter books together, taking turns reading each night. Or if she had a book she was reading for school, we would alternate reading that together (bonus – this helped a lot with comprehension and fluency).

If you kept this habit up, terrific! Don't stop now; let it morph into whatever kind of reading time allows for you. If you stopped because she outgrew story time or other time constraints got in the way, get back to reading together. If you have a specific concern with your tween, perhaps self-image, friend issues, etc., find some chapter books that shine a positive light on these concerns. You may find that not only will she gain some perspective, she may use this time to open up to you about her own struggles. Nothing too heavy, though, or you can't claim that you found this idea in the bright and sunny chapter!

If your evenings are a zoo with the needs of many family members, be creative. When a friend overheard Kendall telling her daughter about a book we were reading together, she lamented that she didn't have time for such a luxury because their evenings were busy cleaning up dinner, finishing up homework, and then baths and stories for the younger children in their family. I suggested that her and her tween pick out some stories and read them together to the younger kids at bedtime. Once they found some books that weren't too "kiddish," they actually found that they loved this activity, and it thrilled the little kids. Because they were young, their attention spans only allowed several minutes of reading, which I'm told was all they needed (and all they had). This short amount of time all together allowed everyone to mellow out, and spend the last few minutes of the day together. Feel free to rope dad in, too, if this is an option.

Girls Days or Nights Out

When time is a hot commodity, it can be hard to carve out time for some girl time away from the house. But with some planning, it can totally be done. And it is so nice to spend some time with your tween away from housework, homework, siblings, and whatever else fills up your day. I have three siblings, and every once in a while my parents would arrange an outing where we could act like an only child – just one child being taken out to dinner without my brother spitting ice on the rest of us, without the arguing over who ate the last chip from the basket, and all of the other chaos that goes along with going out to dinner as a family. I still remember those outings, having all of my parents' attention, and loving it! (And for the record, it was probably me who ate the last chip.)

If you have time, of course it would be nice to do a day of shopping and dinner out. But if you are short on time, and who isn't, then maybe go for a manicure and/or pedicure, a run to the ice cream shop, or to the bookstore or library to pick out some books together (see what I did there?!). You don't need me to tell you what fun outings might appeal to you and your tween. But sometimes we tend to over-think it, and feel that unless we have a solid block of time and a spectacular agenda that it isn't possible to get out together. Lower your expectations and remember that she will thrive on the time with you, not the setting you choose.

Talk About Boys

I'll bet you were wondering when I would talk about boys, and I'll bet you didn't think it would be under the heading of a fun and light topic! All girls have their unique personalities, some have been boy-crazy since preschool, and some have paid little attention to the boys around them. During the earlier tween years, even if there is some boy-craziness, the concept of boyfriends and girlfriends is not often a big issue. The later tween years tend to see considerable amounts of crushes, some announcements of "going out," and even a date or two. My take on all of this? Not a fan. Oh, I don't mind the crushes, and realize that I couldn't stop them if I tried. But research suggests that dating at younger ages is related to increased problematic behavior (36).

If you have already let your daughter begin dating, you are probably mad at me now, and I can handle that. I am simply unwavering in my position on dating as a tween. I have had to bite my lip once or twice when a friend or acquaintance has talked about her tween going on a date. And had to hold back many sarcastic comments when one friend commented that the only movie out that the little daters could get into was "Wreck it Ralph" (shouldn't that be telling us something??). But we can't ignore the reality that most tweens will take an interest, in one form or another, in boys. So my standpoint on this is to make it fun, positive, and a way to connect.

When Kendall was in kindergarten, she came home one day and informed us that a boy in her class had a crush on her. My husband declared then and there that not only was she not allowed to have a crush on any boys, no one was allowed to have a crush on her. While I thought about how we could possibly enforce this, I realized two things. First, when it came time for her to actually date, he would likely need to be sedated. Second, I didn't want to spend the next several years telling her what she could *not* do when it came to relationships with boys. I wanted instead to lay the groundwork for healthy relationships and focus on what she could do.

If you have a boy-crazy girl, my suggestion is to minimize the focus on boys, but be able to respond to her frequent, perhaps incessant, gushes about boys she knows or sees on television. If you respond to the constant stream of comments with replies such as "you are too young to worry about boys," or "why don't you focus more on school," you will do little to stop this trait. And if your tween has a stubborn streak, you don't need me to tell you that this will probably just reinforce her behavior. Instead, ask her things like "oh, you think (insert celebrity crush name here) is cute? I can see why! Is that what you hope your boyfriend looks like?" Or if she's talking about the crush she has in her class, approach it with "the rule in our house is that you can begin dating someone at 15, do you think you'll still like him then? How do you think he might look different then?" This makes your point without being confrontational, and also allows you to have a light-hearted conversation with her. Besides leaving little room for surprises about dating rules in the future, it sets the tone that talking with you about boys is not the start of a fight, and could even be a little fun! The bonus is that you get a sneak peek at what type of boy she is expressing an interest in.

If your tween is not yet bubbling over with an interest in boys, you certainly don't want to create a little groupie. But in the same way that you can use light-hearted banter with her to lay the groundwork for dating later on, you can begin to find out what her group of friends is talking about, because even though she may not yet show an interest, it's likely that some of her friends are. Kendall fell more into this category, she was never very interested in boys. She didn't mind her friends' continual rants about different boys in their class and in the neighborhood, and the boy bands – don't even get me started on the boy bands, but she only somewhat understood what was so interesting. And as she got older and better understood what was so interesting, she still couldn't bring herself to care as much as they did.

A lot of what I did during the non-boy-crazy years is listen to what was going on in Kendall's social circle regarding boys. When it was rumored that another girl in the class was kissing boys Kendall and her friends were appalled – good. When I heard about some of the trashy television shows and PG-

13 movies that her friends were watching – didn't love it, but duly noted. When Kendall reported that one of her friends knew the blood type of every member of One Direction – um, what? (But falling in line with making the concept of boys fun, we sure did get a laugh out of that!)

You get my drift, I paid attention to what was going on, but didn't need to say a whole lot. I would ask random questions, such as seeing a boy crossing the street wearing ridiculously saggy pants, and say "what do you think dad would do if a guy came to the house to pick you up for a date dressed like that?" Again, I don't want to create a focus on boys, but little by little set the foundation for what our expectations, and hopefully her preference, are for the qualities of a potential boyfriend. (By the way, her answer to the question was that she would send the guy home to change before dad could ever "get a hold of him.")

Keep a List

Usually there is nothing fun about my to-do lists. But I do keep one that I love – it's a list of things to do with Kendall. I started doing this during summer breaks when there were so many things that she wanted to do over the summer, but I was afraid we would forget some of them or not make time for them in the midst of a busy sports schedule. Over time, this has evolved into more of a master list of things that I think of to do with her or things that she comes up with. This may seem overly simple, but I'm sure you can relate to having an idea of a fun outing or activity, and then not being able to recall it when you have some free time. With such busy lives, it's nice to be able to have ideas on paper to refer to instead of blank stares and blank minds. Just keep a running list of activities, and if you hear about something you think would be fun or your tween (or any child) mentions a fun idea, jot it down!

Topic Basket

Last but not least, remember the suggestion to keep a basket full of conversation starters and topics on the kitchen table? Keep some light-hearted topics in there as well. After a long day, it's easy to spend dinner focused on who needs a ride where, who forgot to feed the dog that morning, what teacher was out to get your child that day, etc. So not only is the topic basket a fun way to guarantee some positivity, having a mix of topics will ensure that your tween, and family, will come to expect some thought-provoking questions along with some on the silly side. I'll wrap this chapter up, and list a bunch of topics at the end. Obviously, I encourage you to come up with some of your own, but this will get you started.

Have you ever planned a visit to a local theme park with your children? You pack a bag full of snacks and drinks, sunscreen, maybe sweaters, maybe umbrellas, map out your route, remember money for parking, etc. You brave the lines trying to keep everyone entertained. At some point, you finally remember that this is supposed to be fun! Or perhaps it isn't until you see smiles on your kids' faces that you realize that you were so worried about making sure everything went smoothly that you forgot the original intention of the trip.

There are many similarities here. There is no escaping the fact that the tween years involve obstacles that require serious attention and conversations. It can be exhausting to confront all of the challenges that face our tweens – especially when you read a book full of these issues! But don't forget that the most important factor in being able to successfully navigate these issues is a healthy connection with your daughter. And an important part of that is the laughter and joy of being together. Yes, I want you to be aware of the influences that may affect your daughter and be an active participant in mitigating their impact. But I don't want you so weighed down with the negatives that you forget to incorporate a healthy dose of light-hearted interactions into your lives.

Kendall's Corner: Now I'm assuming you know that us tweens aren't thinking of how we can spend time with our moms every second of every day. That's where you as moms come in. My mom creates a list with me at the beginning of summer of things we want to do together. That is just one way to make sure you spend time together, but I know it made my summer a whole lot more fun!

Conversation Starters:

Who is the funniest person in your class? Why?

What did you do today that made you proud of yourself?

What was the nicest thing that happened to you today?

What was the funniest thing you saw or heard today?

Who ate the grossest lunch today (that of course you didn't make fun of)?

How did someone help you today?

Pick a teacher – if you could change one thing about him/her, what would it be?

Who was the best friend to you today?

What are you the most afraid of?

If you could travel anywhere, where would you like to go?

If a movie were made about your life, what actress would you want to play you?

Who should you be nicer to tomorrow?

If you could only eat one food for the rest of your life, what would it be?

If I asked your friends to use three words to describe you, what do you think they would say?

If we could invite one person over for dinner (famous or not, living or dead) who would you pick? Why?

I want you to smile at one person tomorrow who you normally don't talk to – who will that be? Why did you pick that person?

If you were allowed to bring your favorite thing from home to school, no matter what it is, what would you bring?

Think of something awful that could happen – best friends says she hates you, your pants split right down the middle, whatever... name three things you could do to make yourself feel better at the moment it happens, and three things you could do once you get home. (I LOVE this one, gets them to think of some coping skills, this one is a repeat question often at our house.)

Would you rather be forced to say every thought that popped into your head out loud, or never be able to speak again?

Would you rather have to eat a pile of hair or lick the bottom of a stranger's foot?

Would you rather give up your bed or the television (or phone, if they have one)?

If you could redo one 'scene' from your day today, what would it be and what would you redo?

Conclusion:
So Yeah, That's Why
the Need for This Book

I knew that this book would take some time to write, and I thought about it for a while before I really dove in. I knew I didn't want to lose Kendall's perspective, so I had her write her thoughts on certain things so I could capture them in time, because we all know that kids seem to change in the blink of an eye. One of the things I did is have her write a paragraph on what the perfect day would look like for her at different ages. Here is what she wrote at age 9:

> "The perfect day would be with my mom, and we would go to the mall and go into almost every store. Then we would eat lunch somewhere, and after that we take a walk and go to the park. I would feel good and happy!"

What I notice most is that her expectations are fairly low, and friends aren't the main focus. Fast forward a few years, and here is the same assignment at age 12:

> "We wake up at midnight and go out for breakfast. Then we go to New York for two hours and do whatever I want. Then we go to our local theme park and ride anything and get to be the first in line. Then we go and play Mouse Trap. Then I get a laptop and iTouch and the newest iPhone and I do the whole thing with all of my BFFs. I get to stay up all night playing capture the flag with the

neighbors – while the one neighbor I don't like is out of town."

Huh. Something of a different tone, yes? While I'm not specifically mentioned, I must imagine that I am involved only to provide rides and to fund these excursions. While this is, of course, an idealized version of what popped into her head, it does illustrate that what qualifies as fun now involves more material items and a higher level of activity. And mostly, more friends and less mom.

No two tweens are alike, and the differences in tweens from the beginning of this age span to the end can range from subtle to drastic. If you had your tween conduct this exercise, she may have started with a day of playing with dolls all day with you, to ending with hitting the clubs with the Kardashians. Or perhaps there would have been little difference in what her perfect day would be. As I've indicated throughout the book, you know your tween better than anyone, and have the most accurate view of how she is changing during these years, and what will stand out as the most pressing issues to focus on. And it seems that regardless of the disposition of your tween, there never seems to be enough hours in the day to address as many topics as we'd like.

I remember moving into a new home when Kendall was about three years old. She was just about to enter preschool, making some neighborhood friends, and had a swimming lesson or two, but we did not have a very full schedule so our days were filled with walks to the park, coloring, and pretend play. Our neighbors across the street had two boys, around eight and eleven years old. I recall glancing out the window as I would walk past throughout the day, and it seemed that every single time I did, I saw some combination of the boys and their mother or father coming home or leaving in their minivan. All I could think is "where on earth could they possibly have to go this many times during the course of a day?" I joked with their mother about this once, and after sighing a long you're-telling-me breath, she looked at Kendall and said "just wait... you'll see."

She was absolutely right. I don't even remember if commitments slowly accumulated or if they happened all at once, but soon enough school, school functions, lessons, outings with friends, sports, club meetings, and so on kept us hopping – and have only increased. And as much as I'd like to complain, I am amazed at all that Kendall has to do in a day. The amount of work, physical and mental, that is required of her is way more than I could keep up with. Not to mention the expectations of behavior and the things she needs to do at home as well. We ask a lot of our children, and certainly don't want to pile on to the pressures they already face.

It may seem that throughout this book I've asked you to add a daunting amount of time-consuming tasks to your already busy life, but if we do this right, the focus given to the concerns of tweens will actually serve to enhance their lives as well as ours. But I don't want you to feel as if you need to tackle every single issue every single day. I realize that on top of your busy day, adding things such as trying to find time to monitor social media, preview television and music, empower her against bullies, make sure her friends are a positive influence, and have meaningful conversations with your daughter seem like a remote possibility. It will not likely look neat and tidy (but if you do manage to have a flawless day of parental genius, the rest of us don't want to hear about it, okay?) As with so many things in life, this is an endeavor in which you do the best you can.

The teen years are just around the corner. Popular culture suggests that teenagers are infinitely more challenging than their younger counterparts, with increased interest in dating, more reliance on peer influence, and added independence once they are able to drive. I reluctantly agree that this is true, but don't want to suggest that once your tween becomes a teen the sand in your influence-hourglass will run out. It is completely in the realm of possibilities to maintain a wonderful relationship with your teen. Even so, I wrote this book and chose to focus on the tween years as a time to concentrate not only on what can make these years great, but what can fortify your daughter for the years to come.

Above all, I hope you look back at the previous chapters and realize a couple of things. First, there are no extraordinary measures or complicated formulas required in parenting tweens. The most important aspect of being an effective force in her life is her relationship with you. If you have a relationship that contains trust, open communication, and enjoyment, you already have the foundation to manage everything that will come your way. Next, if you read this book and found that you need to make some changes, they probably aren't a complete overhaul of your life; small changes can make a big difference. Maybe you need to listen a little more to your tween, or maybe you need to oversee more of her online activity. Maybe you know who her friends are, but want to do more to get to know them and their parents better. Or it could be as simple as realizing you need to have a little more fun together!

Finally, the best outcome for me would be that after reading this book, you feel confident about parenting your tween, and that you actually enjoy it! I hope that you found the information, encouragement, or support that you need. And I hope you feel like you made a connection to me and Kendall, because connecting is the best way to really make a concept stick. So I would be thrilled if a few months or even years down the road, you were talking to someone and saying "a friend was telling me the story about...." only to realize it was a story you read in here!

Kendall's Corner: At times, your tween is going to act annoyed by all the times you are trying to spend time with them. Trust me, no matter what they say, they will love it. Also, they are going to roll their eyes when you talk to them about drugs and alcohol but it is still important to talk to them, they will remember what you say more than anyone else. My last piece of advice is that the earlier you get involved with their friends, school, and online stuff, the more "natural" it will be and it will seem totally normal when they get older. My tween years were a blast and your tween's can be too!

References

Chapter 1

1, 2. Neinstein, L., & Kaufman, F. (2002). Normal Physical growth and development. In L. Neinstein (Ed.), *Adolescent Health Care: A Practical Guide, 4th edition* (pp. 165-193). Baltimore: Lippincott, Williams, and Wilkins.

3. http://www.mayoclinic.com/health/hair-removal/an00638

4. http://kidshealth.org/kid/grow/body_stuff/menstruation.html

5, 6, 7. Johnson, S., Blum, R. & Giedd, J. (2009). *Adolescent maturity and the brain: The promise and pitfalls of neuroscience research in adolescent health policy.* Journal of Adolescent Health, 45(3), 216-221.

8. Walker, E. (2002). *Adolescent neurodevelopment and psychopathology.* Current Directions in Psychological Science, 11(1), 24-28.

9. Spear, L.P. (2002). *Neurobehavioral changes in adolescence.* Current Directions in Psychological Science, 9(4), 111-114.

10. Joinson, C., Heron, J., Araya, R., Paus, T., Croudace, T., Rubin, C., Marcus, M., & Lewis, G. (2012). *Association between pubertal development and depressive symptoms in girls from a UK cohort.* Psychological Medicine, 42(12), 2579-2589.

Chapter 3

11. Seitz, V. (2007). The Impact of media spokeswomen on teen girl's body image: An empirical assessment. *The Business Review, Cambridge,* (7)2, 228.

12. http://www.pbs.org/newshour/extra/features/health/july-dec12/EatingDisorder-StoryPDF.pdf

13. Richins, M. (1991). Social comparison and the idealized images of advertising, *Journal of Consumer Research,* 18, 71-83.

14. Martin, M. & Kennedy, P. (1993). Advertising and social comparison: Consequences for female preadolescents and adolescents, *Psychology and Marketing,* 10(6), 513-530.

15. Hartmann, T. & Klimmt, C. (2006). Gender and computer games: Exploring females' dislikes. *Journal of Computer-Mediated Communication, 11*(4), article 2. http://jcmc.indiana.edu/vol11/issue4/hartmann.html

16. Anderson, C. & Dill, K. (2000). Video games and aggressive thoughts, feelings, and behavior in the laboratory and in life. *Journal of Personality and Social Psychology,* 78, 772-90.

17. http://www.aap.org/en-us/advocacy-and-policy/aap-health-initiatives/Pages/Media-and-Children

Chapter 5

18. Wiseman, R. (2009). *Queen Bees and Wannabes: Helping Your Daughter Survive Cliques, Gossip, Boyfriends, and the New Realities of Girl World.* New York: Random House.

Chapter 6

19. www.stopbullying.gov

Chapter 7

20, 21. www.stopbullying.gov

Chapter 8

22, 23. www.stopbullying.gov

24.
http://www.isafe.org/outreach/media/media_cyber_bullying

25. Snell, P. & Englander, E. (2010). Cyberbullying victimization and behaviors among girls: Applying research findings in the field. *Journal of Social Sciences*, 6(4), 510-514.

Chapter 9
26, 28, 29. Sheff, D. (2013). *Clean: Overcoming addiction and ending America's greatest tragedy.* New York: Houghton Mifflin Harcourt.

27. Siegel, M., Johnson, R., Tyagi, K., Power, K, Lohsen, M., Ayers, A., & Jernigan, D. (2013). Alcohol brand references in U.S. popular music, 2009-2011. *Substance Use & Misuse. 48*(14), 1475-1484.

30. The Partnership at Drugfree.org sponsored by MetLife. Released April 2011. *Partnership Attitude Tracking Study.* Partnership for drug-free kids. Retrieved from http://www.drugfree.org.

31. *Drug and alcohol fact sheet.* Partnership for drug-free kids. Retrieved from http://www.drugfree.org.

32. Branstetter, S., Low, S., & Wyndol, F. (2011). The influence of parents and friends on adolescent substance use: A multidimensional approach. *Journal of Substance Use, 16*(2) 150-160.

33. *Ten tips for prevention for parents*. National Council on Alcoholism and Drug Dependence, inc. Retrieved from http://www.ncadd.org.

34. Peterson A., Leroux, B., Bricker, J., et al. (2006). Nine-year prediction of adolescent smoking by number of smoking parents. *Addict Behavior. 31*(5), 788–801.

Chapter 10

35. Lovorn, M. (2008). Humor in the home and in the classroom: The benefits of laughing while we learn. *Journal of Education and Human Development*, 2(1).

36. Connoly, J., Nguyen, H., Pepler, D., Craig, W., & Jiang, D. (2013). Developmental trajectories or romantic stages and associations with problem behaviours during adolescence. *Journal of Adolescence*, 36(6), 1013-1024.

Acknowledgements

Debi would like to thank the following people for their invaluable help in the writing of this book:

To Pat, for always making me feel like a great mom, even when you're doing things like begrudgingly sneaking around the neighborhood, stalking our daughter on her first unsupervised trick-or-treat outing so I wouldn't worry so much. Kendall is so lucky to have you for a dad, your energy and love for her is clearly seen in her confidence and her smile. And I am lucky to have you as my best friend and husband. Thank you for always giving me the unconditional support I need to be the mom that I have always wanted to be. Thank you for keeping the fun and laughter alive in our family.

To Dad, the best editor there is! Oh, I know, don't overuse exclamation points. Who knew after years of reviewing my book reports all through school that you would be willing to take this on! (Darn, I did it again with the exclamation points.) I loved having you be such a big part of this book, and loved knowing that you would not pull any punches (I suspected this ever since I got my third grade book report on *Nancy Drew* back from you covered in red marks). You taught us to be reliable, responsible people, and that stupid is never cool. You were dependable as a provider, but also in how you had fun with us. We knew when it snowed it was only a matter of time before you took us sledding, and when it was summer, you would take us swimming once you got home from work.

To Mom, everything I know about being a mom I learned from you, but I don't know if I can ever top your "momminess." Where I have a conscious awareness of the need for balancing nurturing, fun, and guidance, you seemed to have that balance down intuitively. What I know for sure about you is that you were meant to be a mom, and we are blessed to have you as our mom. Sure, being a busy mom of four meant that instead of writing my name on my lunch bag you wrote down whatever you were serving us for breakfast that morning (don't worry, people have finally stopped calling me "Frosted Flakes"). I don't know how you did it, but I do know that we never doubted for a second how much we were loved. I can only hope that Kendall looks back at her childhood and feels even close to the same way.

To Kendall, it's hard to put into words how much I love you. You continue to amaze me every day with your kind heart, your sweet personality, and your funny comments that I never see coming. You do things daily that make me and daddy proud, and I hope make you proud of yourself. You are meant for great things in this world, and it is a better place because you are in it. Maybe now you'll let me kiss you in public? No? It's cool – I tried.

To Kim, Jennie, and Brad, this book would lack a bunch of the funny stories without you guys. With you all, I have learned that a happy childhood is the best gift you can give a child. I also learned that without a sense of humor, life with three siblings would be difficult. And I also learned that you'd better wake up really early if you want to get any of the good cereal. You guys have been amazing aunts and an uncle to Kendall; that means so much to me.

To Dr. Lisa Ingram, I can't thank you enough for your help and input in key parts of this book. I appreciate your time, and I appreciate your friendship. I have been impressed time and again over the years watching you overcome so much and never losing your strength as a mother.

Kendall would like to thank the following people:

To my dog Claire, thank you for being there for me for inspiration and the occasional back rest to write on. I can't imagine my life without you and I love how you help me with my writing even though you don't speak.

To Mom, thank you for letting me be a part of this book. This has been such a fun (and long) process. I wouldn't have wanted to do it with anyone else. I love you. ☺

To Dad, thank you for being there for me and for being a great coach. Thanks for always helping me with my math. And mom and I tried to keep you out of the puberty conversations, so anything you heard better teach you to not eavesdrop again. Oh and thanks for keeping mom happy because when mom's happy everything goes a lot smoother around here.

About the Authors

Debi Smith-Racanelli has earned her Bachelor's Degree in Human Services, a Master's Degree in Psychology, and completed advanced graduate studies in psychology and gender studies. She has clinical experience in counseling settings and non-profits, where she has come to appreciate the importance of effective parenting, and is a passionate advocate of parenting education. She lives in the suburbs of Denver, Colorado with her wonderful husband Pat, who refers to himself as her "extended case study," her fantastic daughter Kendall, and sweet dog Claire.

By the time of publication, Kendall Racanelli has somehow become a teenager. She is a dedicated student and volunteer, competitive softball player, and Denver Broncos and Colorado Avalanche fan. She also enjoys cooking and photography, with her primary subject being her dog, Claire (after selfies, of course).

Made in the USA
San Bernardino, CA
22 June 2018